CW00323150

DANA

with

Lucy Elphinstone

HODDER AND STOUGHTON
LONDON SYDNEY AUCKLAND TORONTO

British Library Cataloguing in Publication Data

Dana.
Dana: an autobiography.
1. Dana 2. Singers – Ireland – Biography
I. Title II. Elphinstone, Lucy
784.5'0092'4 ML420.DI/

ISBN 0-340-42665-9 Pbk

 Printed in Great Britain for Hodder and Stoughton Limited, Mill Road, Dunton Green, Sevenoaks, Kent by Richard Clay Limited, Bungay, Suffolk. Photoset by Rowland Phototypesetting Limited, Bury St Edmunds, Suffolk. Hodder and Stoughton Editorial Office: 47 Bedford Square, London WC1B 3DP.

Acknowledgments

I would like to thank all the people, both family and friends, who have helped me with this book, in particular Lucy for all her hard work, patience and support.

Illustration Acknowledgments

Prizes from the feis – by courtesy of the Belfast Telegraph
Dana and her brothers – by courtesy of the BBC
Relaxation on a bicycle – by courtesy of the Sunday News
TV Christmas – by courtesy of the BBC
Dana with Grace – by courtesy of A. Markey, Daily Mirror
Dana and Kurt Kaiser – by courtesy of Brian Aris, Scope Features
Snow White – by courtesy of Mel Figures
A Star line-up – by courtesy of Doug McKenzie, Professional Photographic Services
Family and friends – by courtesy of Cyril Cain, Daily Mirror
Dana with Damien and family – by courtesy of The Society for the Protection of Unborn Children

1

Everyone looked bigger than me. At six years old, I was small for my age anyway, and the other children in the talent contest all seemed older. Most of them probably were. The competition in Derry's St Columb's Hall was open to all ages and there were no classes. This was my first contest and I was last in the programme. I'd never sung in front of so many people before. The hall was absolutely full and I waited with a kind of nervous excitement for my turn. My hair seemed drawn back too tightly into its stiff pigtail so that my scalp ached, and my fingers felt hot and clammy as I shifted from one foot to another. I could hear my heart pounding in my ears whenever silence fell for another child to perform his piece. Somewhere in the audience I knew my mother would be sitting, small and neat, leaning forward slightly to get a better view as each child hurried nervously on to the stage. I could imagine her head tilted thoughtfully to one side as she assessed each performance.

"Just do your best," she'd told me. "It doesn't matter if you don't win. Just do your best."

Suddenly it was my turn. I walked quickly to the middle of the stage and launched into my song, staring hard at the luminous exit sign at the back of the hall. I knew Mum would be miming the words silently with me just as she did for all her children in these competitions. I was singing an Irish lullaby my granny had taught me and there was no accompaniment. I could feel I was frowning slightly as I concentrated on reaching that difficult high note and remembering the words. In a flash it was over and I padded off thankfully to wait for the results with the other children. The audience had to judge, writing their choice on bits of paper, so it took quite a time for all the votes to be gathered and counted. The results were announced in reverse order, and I was only slightly disappointed and not at all surprised when third and second places were read out and I realised I hadn't made it to the final three. Then to my amazement I heard, "And the winner is . . . Rosemary Brown!" A thrill of excitement shot through me. I'd never won anything before. In fact, I don't think I'd done anything particularly noteworthy at all, so I was gaping like a fish as someone took my hand and led me back on to the stage. The audience didn't seem half so scary when they were clapping hard and full of smiles. I scanned the rows eagerly to find Mum's beaming face.

Little did I think that twelve years later I would win a competition which would be watched by at least 75 million people. But if you live in Derry, maybe it's not such a surprise . . .

Derry is famous for two things. First, for the shirts made there, and second, for the way the people love music. My parents depended on both. When they were growing up, times were very, very hard. There was little work for the men, so it was up to the women to go out and scrape a living working long hours in the shirt and pyjama factories. With life such a struggle, music was the one thing which made it bearable. My father and his brother Johnny were just youngsters when they started playing in the local brass band, and my mother used to follow it round the city with the other children. Her own father played the flute, and all his family were in a flute band. Most evenings were spent singing and playing, though often things were too bad even to bother about making music. Mum started piano lessons when she was about ten, and even though she had to stop three years later, she had already developed a real love for music.

That was what drew my parents together. To them, life

without music would be like bacon without eggs. My father was a barber by trade and he'd make up his money by playing trumpet in a dance band at night, but a few years after they married, Dad was forced to go to London to look for work. Eight months later, Mum with my elder brother Robert and sister Eileen joined him after he had managed to get a job on British Rail, and rent a place down by the docks. Work wasn't much more secure over in England just after the war, but soon he was lucky enough to land a permanent job as a coalman, and they rented a house in Islington just as their fourth child, Susan, came along, following the tragic death of my sister Grace at eight months old.

Right from the beginning they loved it in London. The people were so friendly, and my parents have very warm memories of those early years. Like the first day they moved into their new home – with not a stick of furniture or even a kettle to make a cup of tea. Their neighbours arrived to greet them with a home-made cake and a pot of tea to welcome them to Frederica Street – and Mum still talks about VE Day, so vividly that I almost feel as if I was one of the thousands who ran and danced their way to the celebrations outside Buckingham Palace in the brilliant May sunshine. Uncle Hughie, Mum's brother, was there, playing his old squeeze-box like there was no tomorrow until finally – to the great amusement of everyone present – it fell apart in his hands. When they arrived home in the evening with aching feet and sore throats from all the cheering and singing, neighbours and friends sat out on the steps of the terraced houses while Dad played all the favourite tunes on his trumpet. Melodies like "Cherry Pink and Apple Blossom White" and "O my Papa". Dad was a beautiful trumpet player and Mum said they all sat there listening and singing till it was nearly dawn.

I can remember Frederica Street very clearly. Big wrought iron rails guarded the front of our house. High above them, three storeys reared like a tower over the long grey pavement which peered down in turn into the basement kitchen. I was born in that house, the fifth child, and spent my first five years there. John arrived two years later. The youngest member of the family, Gerald, delayed his entrance until we moved back to Derry in 1956.

Our house always seemed to be full of people – as well as us, there were from time to time other members of Mum or Dad's family who had decided to follow their example and move to London, and sometimes they would take in lodgers to help make ends meet. But I remember a sense of happiness and security there. Mum and Dad often say those were among the best years of their lives.

I'm told that I was a quiet child who could play for hours in the corner with my doll – I suppose that's true because ever since I can remember I was happy to play by myself, finding plenty of games and friends out of my own imagination. (As I got older, I was to be known as the dreamer of the family.)

In fact, for all of us, being creative and providing our own amusement was something that came naturally. In Derry it is in the very air you breathe, and with its music being as much a part of life as eating, the Derry culture coloured our years in London and our house was always full of musicians. It was tradition back home for boys to go into brass bands, and Dad had carried on playing the trumpet in them ever since his initiation into that magic world playing the "clappers" (cymbals) at the age of four. Since it wasn't the thing for girls to be puffing away on tubas and trombones, most of them took up dancing, singing and other musical instruments from a very early age. My parents and relations were all particularly keen, teaching me wee songs long before I could understand all the words. And although I didn't start proper music lessons until I was about six, I used to lie awake at night drinking it all in as the grown-ups sang and played into the early hours.

I have some vivid memories of those years in London. One is of my friend, Loopy Lou, who lived over the street and had a doll's-house in the attic where we played for hours. Another is of a black and white dog-tooth check coat which belonged to my mother. I remember standing at the window one day, crying and crying as I watched her disappearing down the street to do some shopping. But Dad put all to rights by taking my hand and saying, "Your Mummy's not gone out. Look, here's her coat," and opening the cupboard door, he showed me the garment that seemed inseparable from my Mum. I calmed down immediately.

Life was never dull. My dad was very generous, to the point where surprises and treats became traditional in our family. Every Friday night he would take the three oldest children, Robert and Eileen and Susan, to the pictures, treating them to piping hot bags of chips and pickled onions on the way home, not forgetting to buy some chocolates for Mum at the same time (they're still her big weakness). I would be woken up by the sound of muffled giggles on the doorstep, and high, excited voices probably giving a jumbled account of the film to Mum. Then Eileen and Susan would wriggle into bed beside me, and we would drift off to sleep, my nose twitching with the magical aroma of pickled onions and chips!

We three shared a bed until I was about twelve, and Eileen had the best position on the outside, Susan was next to the wall, and yours truly was always squashed in the middle. Eileen was meant to be in charge, and as I was the smallest, I always accepted her authority, but Susan was a free independent spirit who hated to be told what to do, especially by Eileen. They seemed to save all their arguments for bedtime when they were away from Mum and Dad's eagle eyes, and I was for ever getting an elbow in the ear as Eileen lunged across to clout Susan on the arm. After three or four blows, I would quietly crawl underneath the bedclothes down to the bottom and stick my head out the other end. It usually took quite a few minutes before my sisters began to wonder where Rosemary had got to.

With a growing family, there was never much money to spare, but my parents gave us the best of what they had. What we lacked in material things was always made up for by all the attention and time they gave us and the ingenious surprises they conjured up – like on Christmas morning. I would wake up before dawn on Christmas Day, curling my toes in anticipation as I wondered if the same spell as last year would have been cast over the house in the middle of the night. As soon as I heard the first noises in the street, I would slither out of bed and creep softly downstairs, my fingers fumbling for the light switch as my feet touched the cold of the kitchen floor. I can remember the shiver of delight that ran down my spine when I saw that it had happened again. The walls had miraculously changed colour! Instead of yesterday's white, the kitchen was now glowing with a bright new coat of yellow. It was better than any present.

In the same way, Mum seemed able to work wonders with our clothes and appearance. Sewing, altering, mending, she made sure that all of us looked as smart as new buttons when we lined up in front of her appraising eye each morning. And at the end of the day, she would wash, dry and iron our clothes so that our kitchen looked like a refugee camp with skirts, trousers and dresses hanging in every corner.

Our behaviour was watched as carefully as our dress. My parents were both strict, with traditional values and a strong sense of religious duty. They talked about God in a very natural, down to earth way and from an early age we were taught the importance of daily prayer. We'd sometimes say the Rosary together as a family with all the children kneeling meek as cherubs in a row on the kitchen floor. Unfortunately we had a habit of developing uncontrollable fits of giggles. The muffled explosions, thinly disguised as sudden attacks of coughing, were swiftly squashed by Dad or Mum, but most times we could see a twinkle of laughter behind the stern frowns for I'm glad to say they both had a good sense of humour, something which I believe we've all inherited. Going to Mass on Sunday was a family event and as natural as having breakfast. Most of our friends and relatives were Catholic too. In fact we'd generally see most of them at church, but you know, I never remember my parents ever down-grading anyone else's beliefs and they were careful that we inherited that openness and acceptance too. Robert and Eileen attended a non-Catholic primary school in London and my father talked to us often of his Scottish cousins. They were Presbyterian and he was very close to them and very proud of them. So I grew up accepting religion as an essential and natural part of life, with God as a comforting presence who gave security and structure to our lives.

We moved from London because Susan had a bad bronchial chest as a young child and spent many months in hospital. Eventually the doctors decided that she'd be better with the purer air of Derry, so when I was five and a half we moved back to Ireland and settled in the smart new council estate called the Creggan, a couple of miles from the city centre. We loved it. It was a peaceful and attractive place to live, set high on a hill overlooking the city. Dad opened a barber's shop on the estate, and I went to the Holy Child's Infant School just opposite. The day we moved into our new house, some big girls decided to show me the nearby shops but I thought I was being kidnapped and screamed all the way there.

Then, two years later, we moved down the road to Greenwalk, into a larger house opposite the new St Mary's High School, overlooking the big public field half a mile wide where the children played and all community events took place. Every August 15th, there would be a huge bonfire on the green, and everyone would turn out to watch the display. But the highlight of the evening wasn't so much the fireworks as the music and singing. Far into the night, the air would be filled with the haunting strains of "camarlies", old, old Irish folk songs, and the flickering light of the bonfire would be caught in the glistening eyes as the melodies swung from ballads to jigs. This was *my* music, the music that seemed just right to my dreamy nature, and awoke vivid pictures in my mind of beautiful times gone by. When everyone started dancing, I was swept away into another world of excitement and romance.

There was a tremendous sense of community on the Creggan. Most people were Catholics, but as I've said my parents never made any distinction between "Us" and "Them", the Protestants. In my early years I was quite unaware of the tensions that were later to tear our town apart. My mother was very caring and generous towards anyone in need. She could never pass a down-and-out on the street without giving him some money, however little. She'd say, "There but for the grace of God . . ." We were taught to be caring too. A woman across the green from us had an incredible number of children, twenty-two to be exact ("Enough for two football teams," Mum always said), and every Christmas Mum would make us gather up our old toys, and even some new ones, and take them over along with a Christmas pudding or a cake. I used to love wrapping up the presents to make them as exciting and interesting as possible. It never occurred to us to resent parting with our treasures, and any regret at losing a toy was made up for by the happiness and gratitude of the woman. There was no false pride or humility amongst the people on the estate, and both giving and receiving were done with generosity and gladness.

Of course we had our rows there too! My sister Susan was a real ringleader and she'd organise fights between the children. There would generally be two teams of five or six and each child would fight in turn with a member of the other team until two finalists would meet to decide the champion, who invariably was either Susan or Maureen McGilloway. She'd try to rope me into this competition too, but I'd generally end up watching – this was one of the better side-effects of having migraine as a child.

I think I was aware that we hadn't much money, but we were taught to be generous with what we had. For example, Mum regularly gave her last few shillings into the offertory at church, drumming it into us that what you gave you would always receive back in other ways. And time after time, we saw she was right when some money would arrive unexpectedly just when a bill needed to be paid, or Uncle Patrick would come back with us for breakfast after Mass, and slip us children half a crown each, a fortune which would keep us two weeks in sweets and treats. "There you are. Never think you're too poor to give," she would say. Other Christian denominations call this "giving to the Lord" but to Mum it was the same thing as she saw God as inseparable from the Church.

People talked about God and the angels and saints as they would talk of their friends. My grandmother, who also lived in Derry, told me of someone she knew who lost a ten shilling note. She had been searching for it high and low all morning, and when my grandmother called on her, she found the old lady standing in front of a picture of the Virgin Mary, wagging her finger and saying crossly, "This is your last chance, I'm warning you, your last chance!"

"What do you mean?" asked my grandmother, curiously, to which her indignant friend replied, "I've been asking her to help me find my ten shilling note for the past three hours. I can't afford to lose it and I've told her now that if she doesn't find it in half an hour, I'm finished with her!" That was what prayer was like to them. Conversation.

The saints were prayed to for specific problems, each one being particularly good or effective in a different area. One saint might be especially helpful in sickness, another in travel, or in money matters. This was because they were meant to have overcome some adversity in this area in their mortal lives, and were now reckoned to have special understanding and power in intercession in their spiritual state. As children, we were encouraged to see the saints as people who had experienced the same problems we go through, living examples who had suffered and come out the other side with God's help. They were friends who could be asked to intercede or help, but who never took the place of God. He was always represented as the source of all power and love. Except for the picture that hung in my bedroom. It was a painting of Jesus with a very mournful, troubled face, and at night it used to scare the life out of me. As I lay staring at it in the gloom, it looked as if He was winking at me. But on the whole that didn't put me off God – just the artist!

Lily Kerr was my best friend. She also had the most beautiful hair in the world. Ever since those days, I've always longed for long auburn curls, but as I had to make do with my own mousy brown locks, it seemed the next best thing to have Lily as my bosom pal. It was a bit like having your own private film star, especially when we used to sneak out our mothers' high-heeled shoes, hats and handbags, and totter precariously round the streets of the Creggan.

One warm July afternoon, Lily and I were sitting in the middle of the green, solemnly taking tea with imaginary tea-cups and saucers. Lily was dressed in a cheeky little number borrowed from her mother's courtship days, a scarlet blouse with plunging neckline and huge black polka dots, which kept slipping accidentally but to striking effect off her left shoulder. I had gone for a more casual look, with an old green blouse with leg-of-mutton sleeves which fell about six inches below my hands so that I had great difficulty wielding my cup with the desired nonchalance. I was trying to make up for this lack of sophistication by wearing my battered straw hat at a rakish angle over my right eye.

The bright summer sunshine was making Lily's hair glow with a thousand chestnut lights, and I was staring at it in fascinated admiration when suddenly my eye was riveted by a new aspect to her coiffure. An enormous earwig was crawling brazenly up one dangling ringlet straight towards Lily's left ear. Panic swept through me. Earwigs were a horror exceeded only by hairy spiders. But friendship and honour had to come before personal safety. Lily must be saved. Without further hesitation, I heaved my handbag into the air and hurled a death blow at the offending creature with all my might. Crash! The handbag caught Lily on the back of the head, knocking both Lily and the earwig to the ground.

When she had stopped crying long enough for me to explain the danger she had been in, Lily proved that she had virtues beyond just her beautiful hair. Instead of thumping me back for nearly knocking her unconscious, she clasped my hands tightly and whispered in awe, "You *saved* me, Rosemary. You saved my life. Oh thank you, thank you!"

From that moment, a new bond was forged in our friendship. If she was Lily the Beautiful, then I became Rosemary the

Brave, and we were never to forget the epic earwig-slaying.

By this time I was attending St Eugene's, a girls' primary school in the grounds of the cathedral near the town centre. My grandmother had been reared right opposite and had been to the same school with my great-aunt Mary. They still lived quite close, and I would often stop off to see them after school. It was a long walk to school from the Creggan, and often Susan and I would travel by bus, but the highlight of the day was visiting the tiny sweet shop opposite the school gates. I remember we had one penny of pocket money between us each day. My passion was Walker's toffees, two of which you could buy for a halfpenny, but Susan loved dolly mixtures and always seemed to get a better deal than me with her halfpenny's worth.

2

I was started on official lessons in piano, violin and ballet at the age of six. There were two large festivals every year in Derry, one Irish and one English, and all the surrounding towns would have two as well, with competitions in piano, violin, singing, verse-speaking, dancing. In the Irish "feis", the emphasis would be on traditional Irish folk songs and dances, whereas in the English one the music would be more classical – madrigals and minuets – and the dancing more likely to be ballet. I was entered for all of them, and it was possible to compete in about twenty a year. There was no prize money, but you could win enough medals and cups to start a scrap metal business.

I always think I became a singer really by accident. Ballet was my first love, and I'm eternally grateful to my great-aunt Mary for paying for my lessons since I was six. It wasn't so common at that time for a girl of my religious background to concentrate on ballet as most Catholics went in for traditional Irish dancing. But I just loved the grace and beauty of ballet, and right from a little girl it was my dream to be a ballerina. There was a kind of freedom and joy in ballet and I suppose it was fantasy come to life for me – the beautiful dress and the lovely music. I used to have an imaginary ballerina who lived in my hand, and on long bus journeys I would see her dance and pirouette on my palm.

The trouble with singing for me was that I got so nervous. I was too timid to think I was any good at it. My knees would shake and my stomach get all knotted up so that sometimes I used to think I would either just collapse in fright or be violently sick! I felt much more at ease dancing and acting when I could imagine myself to be anyone other than plain, ordinary Rosemary Brown. I know Aunt Mary always used to say I should become an actress because she said I had the imagination to impersonate anyone. She also used to say that anything I did, I did with all my might, but I think she had a shrewd idea that because I was so nervous and shy I just had to throw myself into it completely or I'd never get out on to the stage. Mind you, she had a very special way of dealing with my nerves. At one feis, I was standing in the wings waiting for my turn in the dancing competition. My stomach, which had been lying somewhere around my knees, now seemed to start floating all over my body, and suddenly I turned to Aunt Mary in panic and cried I couldn't go on. Her reply was to give me two quick thumps and say, "Get out there and dance, girl!" People used to talk about my courage in performing as a small girl, but I think maybe it was more fear of Aunt Mary's hand!

My great-aunt Mary is a very stylish lady – a beautiful singer who had been an exceptional ballroom dancer in her youth. With her brother, my uncle Patrick, she won most of the ballroom dancing contests that were held in Derry and round about. My grandmother, Aunt Mary and Uncle Patrick all sang, inheriting their talent from my great-grandmother Hasson who was Scottish and famous for her exquisite voice. Although Aunt Mary had many suitors she never married but looked after her mother until she died, after that sharing a house with Uncle Patrick. That's perhaps why she gave so much time and attention to her grand-nephews and -nieces – and still does now in her seventies with great energy and good humour. From a tiny girl, I used to spend hours at her house where she would teach me all sorts of dances and songs. The same with my granny. I learnt one song called "Tammy" (Debbie Reynolds sang it, I think, in a show of that name) but that was a big mistake. It became so popular at school that every time the headmistress came into the room, I had to stand up in front of the whole class and sing this song. Terrifying. I used to dread the door opening.

So at the beginning I concentrated on my dancing and left most of the singing to my talented sisters. For my ballet lessons I went to the home of Miss Kathleen Watson and her sister Miss Peggy. Our lessons took place on Saturday mornings in their terraced house in Clarendon Street, in a big L-shaped room which had been two rooms knocked into one. There were practice barres along the mirrored walls, clean wooden floors, a piano, and huge windows at either end looking out on to the garden and the front street. There we learnt Discipline. That was Miss Watson's favourite word for she was always very strict, but she made us work and achieved some remarkable results with the girls who went to her. She would never allow chattering or giggling during a lesson, and would often roar at us, "When I'm explaining something to you, STAND STILL AND DON'T MOVE A MUSCLE! Just listen!" Now, whenever I am being told something in rehearsals, I immediately freeze into Miss Watson's statue with such ease that many producers have commented on my ability to remember exactly the sequence and angles of the shots. I know that I owe this concentration to Miss Watson and her Discipline.

Even though Miss Watson could be quite ferocious at times (when she was trying to give up smoking for three months her temper was fearful!), her bark was worse than her bite. She had a heart of gold underneath and gave us endless encouragement as well as the benefit of her considerable experience and skill. Her pupils walked off with most of the ballet prizes in Derry, but she also taught other kinds of dancing, like tap. The first number I ever performed was called "Strolling" which I did in a snazzy little gold outfit with matching top-hat, cane and gloves. Miss Watson also gave us a lot of practical hints which have stood me in good stead in my later career. She taught me how to walk up and down steps in a long balldress keeping your head erect and without looking at your feet. The secret was to push your foot into the back of the step until the heel touched – a simple thing, but it is surprising how many girls (and adults) ruin the effect of their performance or appearance by yanking their skirts up round their knees and peering anxiously down at the steps.

Although I did ballet, I also grew up with a passion for traditional Irish folk tunes and dances. I used to spend a lot of time at my grandmother's, and she must have taught me hundreds of songs, and a lot of the folklore that went with them. The wonderful stories of leprechauns and fairies set my imagination on fire, and when I sang them I used to get so caught up in the wonder of it that I felt as if I was part of the tale myself.

Someone else who encouraged me no end was the new curate in our parish, Father Edward Daly, later to become Bishop of Derry. He was very keen on the children in the city getting involved in music and dancing, and he organised all sorts of cultural events and competitions, like that first one I took part in when I was six. These competitions were like endurance tests – for the adjudicators! For example, when I was ten, I won the under-elevens girls' singing solo in the Irish feis with an Irish language song, a set piece which had to be performed by every single competitor. There were 120 entrants in my age group! I remember being absolutely dumbstruck when I came first (I had thought the judges must have been asleep by the time my turn came – maybe they were!) but I was thrilled when the adjudicator said there was a "bit of magic" in it when I sang.

I have a great love for my grandmother. For as long as I can remember, I've been comfortable with her. As a child, I'd play dressing up in her funny old clothes and beads, and we would chat for hours. Often I used to stay the night with her, and although she had a spare room we always shared the same bed so that we could carry on talking into the night all snug and warm, which became a tradition with us. The only problem was that Granny used to snore. Usually I could shut her up by giving her a gentle shove with my foot, but one night I just couldn't get her to stop so I gave her a good hefty kick on the shin. Out of the darkness came a stern voice, "Little girl, will you *please* stop kicking me." I got such a fright I shut my eyes quickly and gave a contented little snore myself hoping she would think I was asleep. But my granny isn't easily fooled.

She couldn't play the piano so she used to teach me the songs by ear – but my mum would often tinkle away in the evening when her work was finished, and my sisters and I would sing along with her. That was how we discovered one ingenious way of going to bed later than we should. As soon as bedtime loomed, one or other of us would rush to the piano and start playing the latest tune we were learning. Mum would come in "just for a minute" to hear how we were getting on and invariably she would end up playing the piano and we'd sing. An hour or so later we'd head off to bed – mission accomplished. It was on one of these nights that my mother scared the life out of me by suddenly taking her hands off the keys and whirling round on me: "Rosemary, was that you singing harmony?" I nodded miserably, thinking I must have been out of tune, but instead she said, "That's beautiful, love. You've got a natural gift."

So that was how it was discovered. I hadn't been taught the theory of harmony at that stage. It was just something that came to me instinctively. Now I had a role to play with my sisters, and from that time for a few years we sang as a trio. My father used to organise Christmas concerts for the elderly and mentally handicapped, so we were always singing and dancing in hospitals, homes and church halls. These were great fun because here we could perform popular songs, whereas in the local feises we had to do more serious material. I think this broad training is one of the reaons why I still enjoy and perform such a wide variety of musical styles.

Although Eileen had a beautiful voice and had in fact been offered a lot of work with different bands and groups, she decided to go over to Birmingham to study hairdressing, staying with my aunt and uncle there, so initially that left Susan and me to sing at the festivals and concerts. But that didn't last long either. After hearing a talk on religious vocations at school, fourteen-year-old Susan, the fiery rebel, outspoken and always in trouble, was bowled over and asked to enter the convent. It was not unusual for at least one member of a family to go into the religious life, but Mum was convinced that Susan was too young, and there were several battles before she allowed her to become a novice. Still, she didn't miss out as the education she was given at Bloomfield Convent was excellent. The nuns seemed to bring out a lot in Susan in talent and temperament. We already knew she had a beautiful soprano voice but they discovered that she was a very talented pianist as well and although she didn't go on to take her vows, I think she really enjoyed her time there.

With Eileen busy with her hairdressing, Susan and I spent more time together when she returned from the convent, writing our own songs now and singing in local concerts. We even appeared in a short summer season at the Palladium – in Portrush, Co. Antrim, that is! Susan, introducing a song one night, got in a muddle between Long Player and LP and ended up announcing that the song was recorded on Jim Reeves' last "Long P". After a stunned silence we both collapsed in hysterical laughter – quickly followed by the audience! In 1964, with Susan now a student nurse in Braintree, Essex, the rest of us went to England for the summer as usual, and one of our aunts put Susan and me in touch with a famous music arranger, Frank Barber, who in turn introduced us to Les Perrin. (The latter became press agent for the Rolling Stones and later my own press agent after the Eurovision Song Contest.) They seemed to like our performance, raw though it must have been, and they paid for us to make a demo disc in London of some of the songs we'd written. That caused great excitement, and they had grand plans for a block-busting singing duo. But romance was in the air. Susan, at eighteen, had fallen in love with a young American airforceman, Ronald Stein, who was stationed at Braintree with the American armed forces. Just as we were beginning to see our names in lights, Susan announced that she wanted to get married and go back with Ron to the States.

There was uproar. America might have been on the other side of the universe. People who went there hardly ever came back. It might seem primitive now, but in those days, without phones, and very little money for transatlantic visits, it was like saying goodbye to your loved ones for ever to let them go across the water. Yet somehow, despite the stormy reaction of my parents and the collapse of my own immediate dreams, I strongly approved of their getting married. I was very close to Susan, and I knew how deeply they were in love. At last Mum and Dad consented. Ron, a non-Catholic, converted to our denomination as that was the Church ruling at that time and after a beautiful wedding they were whisked off to a new life beyond the ocean.

Meanwhile, all sorts of religious milestones were being passed in those primary school years. In fact, looking back now I can see that from an early age God was a very real person to me. I remember the time I first realised the significance of the Crucifixion. I was about seven or eight, attending the Good Friday celebrations in the cathedral. Behind the altar was a beautiful stained glass window depicting the Crucifixion and as I knelt staring at it, I suddenly realised that this man had really died a terrible death for me. Tears were streaming down my face, but somehow it didn't matter that people could see my crying. I felt heartbroken.

At about this time I made my first confession. The whole of my primary class lined up, fidgety and nervous in case we'd forget our prayers or get the order of things muddled up. But we had such a lovely priest, Father Brown (no relation!), and he let us make our confession sitting next to him in the pew so that it just seemed like a chat with an old friend.

My first Holy Communion soon afterwards was a great day. My mother made sure that I looked like a little princess in my beautiful white dress and veil. It was a Saturday morning so Mum took me to Miss Watson's afterwards to show the ballet class my lovely dress and tell them about the big event. One little girl looked at me in awe and asked, "Did you just get married today?"

But it was my Confirmation at about the age of ten which was the most nerve-racking of all. We had been primed before the Bishop's visit with a detailed account of what would happen in the ceremony. One of the items was a series of questions on our catechism which he might fire at any of the children. I'd been in all the classes, but I was terrified in case he asked me a question as I was sure my mind would go a complete blank. Luckily, I was sitting almost behind a pillar during that part and he couldn't see me, but the worst was still to come. We had been told that part of the ceremony was for the Bishop to strike each child on the cheek with his ring as a symbol of the challenge to become a soldier of Christ and be prepared to suffer for Him. I knelt in front of the Bishop, flinching, with my face contorted out of all recognisable shape, waiting for that terrible blow. But all I felt was a gentle tap on the cheek so that I looked up, blinking in astonishment, and met two kindly eyes smiling down at me in amusement.

The time was approaching to take the 11-plus exam. I wasn't much looking forward to it as the nuns said I'd be lucky to pass it with so many irons in the fire. Also, Mum and Dad loved England and we spent most summers there with our relatives so occasionally I was late coming back to school, and used to find it hard to catch up on all I'd missed. I had lots of cousins in England I got on really well with, and not seeing them for a year at a time meant we always had masses of news to catch up on and plenty to talk about. Also we could get up to things we couldn't do in Derry.

One of the best of these was exploring the famous Romford market. If we weren't staying with Uncle Patrick and Aunt Mary Rose in Birmingham then we would be with Uncle Brendon and Aunt Pearl (or Uncle Jimmy and Aunt Rosaleen, or Aunt Frances!) in Romford, and it was always a treat to go down to the market with my cousins Kathleen and Jacqueline and our mothers. While they did their shopping, we three would head off on our own, put on mascara and lashings of lipstick, not forgetting the forbidden flesh-coloured tights, and spend the rest of the day imagining ourselves to be cool London jetsetters as we wandered round watching all the bustle, the fascinating stalls and the wonderful characters – and avoiding our parents! When it was time to catch the bus home, we would scrub all our make-up off and appear clean faced and innocent, with our tights carefully hidden in the bottom of our shopping baskets.

Another vivid memory I have of our stays in Birmingham, on the other hand, was catching the bus with Mum from King's Heath to the city centre to shop in the Bull Ring. At least, that was our story. In fact, the real reason for the trip was the little café at the bus stop which sold the best home-made apple pie I've ever tasted. Mum and I used to eat it smothered with custard, the first thing we did when we got off the bus before we could tackle any of the shopping!

Well the nuns were right. The prediction came true. I failed my 11-plus, and I wasn't helped by my old problem of nerves. In the middle of the exam, I just went word-blind. I could not spell "but"! The more I racked my brains, the more a cloud seemed to settle in my head, and after getting stuck on an easy word like that, you can imagine how I went to pieces for the rest of the exam.

But my parents were determined that I should have the benefits of a grammar school education. The nuns themselves said there was nothing the matter with my intelligence, but I was such a dreamer. Still, somehow Mum and Dad raked together the money to send me to Thornhill where I wanted to go more than anything, and I know it must have cost them a good deal of sacrifice. At that time, if you passed the 11-plus, you went to the grammar school free, but if you failed, it was still possible to go as a fee-paying pupil if you passed an entrance exam. In fact, three years later, I took the junior exam and got a scholarship so after that I attended Thornhill free.

3

Thornhill is an imposing Victorian house built of grey stone on a hill overlooking the estuary about four miles from the centre of Derry towards the border. Bought by the Sisters of Mercy in 1932 for use as a convent, it was soon established as a school and classrooms were gradually added in the beautiful grounds. When I first went there in 1963, the school was still quite small, but now there are over 1,400 pupils and many of the peaceful lawns and beautiful rhododendrons have sadly been uprooted to make way for the new classrooms and laboratories.

On the first day my father took my friend Margaret and me to school in the car, as it was a very long bus journey and he wanted to make sure we'd get there. We were very excited and every few minutes we'd ask if we were near the school. When we finally reached our destination and I jumped out of the car I just burst with pride when I heard a woman commenting to her friend, "Just look at the wee Thornhill girl in her lovely uniform!" I felt as if I was the first girl in the world ever to wear the treasured navy blue uniform.

I found the first day a shock though. I was separated from my friends from St Eugene's and we all seemed to go into different classes. At break time, I sat and wept bitterly on some stone steps near the convent because I thought I would never see them again. Luckily I wasn't discovered as I learnt later that those steps were out of bounds. But I soon realised that we weren't parted for ever when I saw that we were shuffled round for different subjects. By the end of the day, I was as thrilled as the rest of them with our new school.

There was a huge rhododendron bush below the house which was so lovely that we called it "Paradise". We were actually allowed to play in it towards the end of my junior years. Where we weren't allowed to play was down by the river, but as we became more bold in the years ahead, some of us used to sneak off through the shrubs to sit by the edge of the water. Although I was quite shy and very scared of the teachers to begin with, I seemed to have a streak of mischief underneath. In fact, the nuns tell me now that I was good as gold one year, and into every kind of trouble the next. I think I remember being naughty a bit more often than that, but maybe I just wasn't caught!

By the time the home bell went at four o'clock on the first day, I was feeling exhausted. We had been issued with the entire books for the first year, and it took Margaret McKeever and me so long to stagger to the bus stop with our burdens that the Creggan bus had left. There was nothing for it but to walk home and off we lumbered.

We were almost crawling by the time we reached the Creggan and our worried parents. It was gone six o'clock and quite dark when we finally dropped our bulging satchels and nursed the angry welts on our hands. There are many sagas I could tell of our adventures simply getting to and from school, particularly in the winter when the Creggan and Thornhill would both be snowbound.

I soon became part of a gang of friends who stayed together all through our years at Thornhill, and even now I keep in touch with them and share some good times. Quite a few of them are related which helped matters as our parents knew each other well and were quite happy if they knew we'd be at one of their houses. There was Blathnaid, and Evelyn McCafferty, her cousin. Maura, Shaun and Pauline McAteer were also cousins, and then there were my own cousins, Seamus, Aileen and Ann Gallagher. There was also Sheila Doherty, Margaret McKeever, Santina Fiorentini, and Roma

Cafolla whose mother was the pianist at the ballet school and my first teacher of the piano and violin. Last but not least was Martin Cowley. The boys all went to St Columb's, the boys' grammar school nearby.

The Beatles hit the school in my first year. All the girls went around with dog-eared photos stuffed covetously into their tunic pockets, and it seemed compulsory to be in love with at least one of them. To be honest, I didn't think any of them were that good-looking – I was still mad on Cliff and the Shadows – but I felt I had to have one of them as my idol. As I stood in the school assembly hall, day-dreaming through the first hymn, I remember thinking coolly, "If I've *got* to be in love with one of them, I'll choose Paul McCartney as he does have lovely eyes."

As we grew into our teens, we became more and more conscious of the pop world and the latest fashions. On Friday evening, we all changed into black stretch trousers, black polo neck sweaters and white Aran cardigans. Later on we became really sophisticated and applied thick layers of Max Factor foundation (the blue tube!) and eye-liner you put on with a brush. I was quite good at doing this, but as I generally applied it as I jogged down into town on the back seat of a bus, it ended up anywhere but on my eyes.

We all had about two shillings and sixpence pocket money a week, and the great thing on Friday night wasn't drinking or dancing, but a huge bag of chips which cost just a shilling. I ended up quite a connoisseur of chips. I started off always liking the long, thick chips, but later I was introduced to the delights of the crispy end bits and I've never looked back. Unfortunately! Clutching our hoard, we would climb over the railings into the children's park near the cathedral when it got dark and munch away, sitting on the swings and roundabouts. I always had to keep half an eye out for the ominous sight of my father's black and white Hillman Minx coming slowly down the road to make sure we weren't up to any mischief. The registration number, VUS 198, is seared on my brain for ever. In fact, it's the only car number I've ever been able to remember! In winter, or when the weather was bad, we would usually go to Evelyn's house almost opposite St Eugene's Primary School, and listen to the Beatles or Cliff.

It must have been one of my "off" years according to the nuns when the whole lot of us decided to "dob" school – play truant, in other words. It was a bit difficult to organise as there were so many of us, but the plan was that we should all set off to school as usual, and then change out of our uniforms in some discreet place, and all converge at Blathnaid's home.

I set out in high spirits with the Gallaghers and Evelyn, and soon we were propping each other up in the gateway opposite Blathnaid's house, giggling helplessly as we struggled to pull off the thick navy stockings. I was just balanced precariously on one leg when Blathnaid came dashing out of her house and led us in a frantic scramble down Francis Street, explaining between gasps that she had just been changing her stockings in the hall, thinking the coast was clear, when her mother had reappeared, and she'd had to pretend she was rushing off to school. But I don't think many people would have been fooled into thinking we were demure Thornhill girls making our way meekly to school. I had one stocking on and one stocking flying like a banner from my right hand as we careered along to the safety of the Gallaghers' house where we were sure everyone was out. I fell through the door with my hair in my eyes and my cheeks the colour of tomatoes. Sheila put us all to shame by turning up soon afterwards already changed and looking, as usual, like something straight out of *Vogue*.

But we were all soon in a fine holiday mood. Most of the morning was spent peeling potatoes to hearty choruses of the latest Beatles' hits, and by midday we were surrounded by bowls of chips. In no time at all, the frying pan was sizzling with load after load of piping hot French fries served up with mounds of marrowfat peas. The smell of chips and vinegar was overwhelming – in our clothing, in our hair, and hanging in heavy clouds all round the house. When we opened the windows, the smoke streamed out in black spirals. That was our downfall. In the middle of what must have been my fourth plate of chips and peas, there was a knock at the door, and immediately pandemonium broke out as we fell over each other trying to hide in the cupboards and under the beds. I ended up in the coalhouse. Somehow Aileen managed to fob off the anxious neighbour with the story that the smoke was just from the spot of lunch she was fixing for her brother and sister who were home sick from school, and we all crawled out to finish our party.

On another day, in a particularly warm summer, we decided it would be almost a sin to stay cooped up in a classroom instead of enjoying God's beautiful creation, so we all hitch-hiked to the seaside at Portrush, about forty miles away on the beautiful Antrim coast. Neither I nor any of the girls had ever hitched before so it was quite an adventure, and on the way out there we were lucky enough to get lifts without any problem. When we arrived on the shimmering stretch of golden sand, we felt as if we'd been transported to some exotic South Sea island, but after a few minutes I discovered that I wasn't enjoying the same holiday spirits as the rest of the crowd. At first I couldn't understand my strange uneasiness. Then I realised it was because my aunt Mary and uncle John Minihan lived in Portrush and I had a nagging fear that I might bump into them, even though they lived on the other side of the bay. So, while everyone else splashed on the suntan lotion, and cooled off in the *extremely* cool Atlantic, I kept looking nervously over my shoulder for the formidable figure of my aunt bearing down upon us. But the day passed without any discovery, and in the late afternoon, sunburnt and tired, we prepared to hitch back to Derry in groups, one of us standing on the roadside thumbing, and two others hiding in the hedge nearby. It seemed as though our luck had run out. The cars streamed past, hardly giving us a glance, all anxious to press on home after a hard day's work or gruelling session on the baking sand. We had to walk miles before someone took pity on us. My feet ached for weeks afterwards – as did my hand with all the lines I had to write out as punishment.

About this time, I met my first boyfriend. Ronnie played in

a group which specialised in Shadows' numbers, complete with all the steps and gestures. His brother Freddy played in the band too, and after my sister, Susan, and I had known them casually for a little while, they asked us to sing with them and we did small charity concerts around the city. It was love at first sight for Ronnie and me, and conveniently Susan and Freddy fell for each other from the start, too. If our parents had known there was any romance in the air, they would have hit the roof, but luckily they thought that all our meetings were in the noble cause of Music, and there was a lot they would allow for that. Ronnie was a really lovely person with a great sense of humour and we were to remain very close until I was about sixteen when our romance drifted to an end.

My first "official" date came then, with one of my friends' brothers, Shaun: he was tall, dark, handsome and witty. I couldn't believe that he'd asked me out. There would often be musical evenings at one of our homes when everyone would bring guitars, on which I had learnt to play three chords in the last few years. We were folk fanatics. Top of my list were Joan Baez and Bob Dylan – and, of course, Irish folk songs.

The other highspots of those days were the "ceilidhs" – mad get-togethers where anything could happen. There was music, dancing and songs but the main feature was Irish dancing in so-called formation. The real attraction of a ceilidh was that none of us had a clue what we were doing, despite the person calling desperate instructions from the front. Merry chaos reigned after the first five minutes, with excitement reaching a peak every time the partners had to swing each other round. Girls would be flying in all directions and collapsing in hysterical heaps at the side of the room. Our interpretation of dances like "The Siege of Ennis" had to be seen to be believed.

These unsophisticated jamborees were all I was allowed until the age of fifteen when my parents let me go with Eileen to my first proper dance. Up till now, despite our relatively sheltered upbringing, my friends and I still considered ourselves the height of fashion. I remember us seeing for the first time a girl with a skirt just above the knee and deciding it was definitely vulgar. The local dance halls were the Embassy in Derry and the Borderland at Muff about five miles outside town, and it was to the latter that Eileen chaperoned me and two friends to have our first taste of real sophistication. Eileen was looking very stunning as usual – she had a great figure and was dressed to perfection in a beautiful circular skirted dress with can-can petticoats, while we three "young ones" sat in the bus, trying not to look too excited, and puffing out our bosoms to make ourselves look a couple of years older. Eileen's beady eye ensured that we couldn't have anything but a very respectable and modest evening, and it was certainly a different world from the hilarious free-for-all of the ceilidhs.

Towards midnight, a very polite young fella asked if he could "leave me home", as the local phrase was, but Eileen was adamant that I should return with her in the bus. Reluctantly I returned to explain the situation to the boy and danced the last set with him, but when the couples began to disperse, there was no sign of Eileen anywhere. I scoured the dance hall and searched outside but when I still couldn't see her I decided I'd better wait for her in the bus. Well, I waited and waited but still Eileen didn't appear. When the bus finally set off for Derry, I concluded with a certain amount of righteous indignation that she must have gone home with someone herself. None too pleased, I yawned my way home with my friends. When I stumbled sleepily through the front door, I was astounded to find no Eileen and two frowning, anxious parents. The whole family sat up watching the minutes ticking by and waiting for the sound of her step outside. At 4 a.m. Dad was just about to get the car out and drive across the town to look for her, when an exhausted and furious Eileen burst through the door. What strength she had left, having apparently walked the eight miles from the Borderland, she used to hurl insults and recriminations at me for my thoughtlessness and stupidity. When she had calmed down a little, it transpired that she hadn't realised I had gone back on to the dance floor for the last dance, and, not finding me with the other girls collecting their coats, she had feared that I had been lured outside by the ravenous wolves, and had hurried out to herd me safely on to the bus. Having searched frantically all round the grounds of the dance hall and then inside once more, she realised that the last bus had gone and, whatever my fate, I had abandoned her, sentencing her to a long and lonely walk home. It was pointless trying to explain my side of the case. All sisterly concern had been squashed out of poor Eileen on the long trudge home and I think she wished someone else had saved her the trouble of resisting the urge to wring my inconsiderate neck.

That was my first and last experience of proper dances for quite a while. My parents labelled me as irresponsible and for some time my only outings were to piano and ballet lessons. In my third year at Thornhill, I was chosen to take the lead in the popular musical *Love from Judy* (*Daddy Long-Legs* as it is known by its other stage name). The show was a great success, but as a result of this and all the festivals I was taking part in at the same time, my academic work suffered, and I had to retake my third year. The staff at Thornhill gave me loads of encouragement, and at the end of it I won the scholarship in the junior exam which rebuilt my confidence.

There was someone who helped me almost more than anyone else at school and especially with my music. She was Sister Imelda. I came into contact with her in my first year at Thornhill when she reported me to the headmistress for talking in chapel, and I marked her down as just a crabby old nun. But after that disastrous start, I began to discover the beautiful personality that lay inside her small bird-like figure, and by the time I reached the sixth form, and she was in semi-retirement, Sister Imelda was one of my closest allies. She taught me music off and on throughout my whole time at school, and we drew particularly close during the school musical when her energy and encouragement inspired us all. I had thought that she was rather severe, but I soon found that she had a tremendous sense of humour. She was also extremely perceptive and caring. If she saw you were having problems about something (and I used to get terrible nerves over my exams, for example), then she would sneak you up to the convent, out of bounds, give you a piping hot cup of tea, and just chat about things. I always left her room feeling the world was a better place.

It was a great sadness to me, then, when Sister Imelda died in March 1983. She had remained a staunch supporter and much loved friend throughout my singing career, and I felt the loss deeply, even though she had been ill for a long time. She had suffered a stroke and could hardly move or talk when I visited her just before she died. She was very frail, but to me she still looked radiant and I couldn't help exclaiming, "Why, you're beautiful, Sister!"

"Now you don't expect me to believe that," she said softly, looking even more lovely as her grey face relaxed into a gentle smile. But when I insisted, she looked suddenly young again as her smile broadened into her familiar mischievous twinkle.

"Well, all right then," she conceded. "Beautiful – except for my feet."

Being educated in a Roman Catholic convent school meant that religion continued a natural part of my life. But at about the age of fifteen I began to doubt all that I had accepted about God – a process which I now believe was an essential part of growing up for me. We had always been taught at school that it was good to question ideas and beliefs so that we really felt the opinions we held were true and not just a load of brainwashing. That was fine so long as it only applied to academic or political ideas, but to doubt the belief which had formed the structure of my whole life was a shattering experience. Every teenager wants some goal or ideal to aim for. For Christianity to be escapism seemed a betrayal of all I felt it should be. I had the awful feeling that religion was just a cop-out, and that God was like a lump of putty; when you had a problem, you took a piece of this God-putty and stuck it over the crack so it looked like new again and you could go happily on your way. Suddenly it all seemed like a cheap joke, a con-trick to fool you into not facing the hardships and problems of life.

These thoughts shook me to my roots, and although outwardly life went on as normal, inwardly I spent a year feeling lost and confused. I was shocked by my own lack of faith and angry at being made to feel a fool. I knew I couldn't talk about it without getting upset and crying, and somehow I felt deep down that this was something I had to sort out completely by myself. Despite all the turmoil inside, I continued going to Mass because some instinct for survival told me that if I felt this bad *with* the structure of discipline, I would feel a thousand times worse *without* it.

At the end of this nightmare year, I went on the usual school retreat which that year was a three-day silent one with prayer and meditation. The tension built up over those three days. God seemed so unreal, and somehow life didn't make sense any more. By the last day, I felt so miserable and confused that when my turn came to take confession, I just broke down and wept. The priest, Father Hamill, was a wise man, and he simply told me to wait outside until he could come out and talk to me properly. When he sat down beside me, out it all came in jumbled bursts, but he seemed to know exactly what was at the root of all my misery. After a few minutes' silence in which he just left me to calm down, he began to talk quietly.

"If what you say is true, that religion is just a sort of drug to keep you feeling good, then being a Christian would be the easiest, happiest state in the world. But living your life in the way God asks you to is the most difficult, challenging thing you'll ever undertake."

I didn't experience a great surge of joy, or dramatic conversion, but what he said made sense, as if I was hearing a record played at the right speed for the first time. I'd known in my head all he'd told me for years, and yet it had all become muddled and meaningless, just empty words rather than a way of life. Gradually I began to realise that faith was not just a habit, a ritual, but a gift from God which we were free to choose or refuse. We received it when we understood that it was bought for us by the death of His Son. In return He asks that we give Him nothing, except our love – and our lives laid down for Him to use to bring His life to others.

I didn't jump into the air shouting "Hallelujah!" or "I've seen the light!" but I knew in my heart that I had made my first real step of personal commitment. To see Christianity as a challenge instead of an escape was a shaft of light. I soon discovered just how much of a challenge. There were some hard times ahead.

4

I had always loved ballet, and despite my singing it had been my ambition either to become a ballerina or to teach dance. In fact when I was fourteen, during one of our summer trips to London, I enrolled as a temporary junior pupil at the Bush Davies School of Dance in Romford and, as I had already passed my grades, I was quickly accepted as a senior pupil with the chance of staying on and taking up ballet professionally. But Mum and Dad felt I was too young to stay in England without them, so reluctantly I had to turn my back on my glittering career. In fact, life as a ballerina probably wouldn't have turned out to be quite so glamorous as I imagined it. Although only five feet four inches, I was still reckoned too tall and beefy for a prima ballerina, and I probably would have been relegated to a life of playing a gawky cygnet in the corps de ballet in *Swan Lake*. Now I finally decided that even teaching ballet was not the career for me either.

In fact a whole new chapter in my life was about to begin.

During the spring of 1965, I was performing in a local talent contest, scheduled to do a dance called "The Bisto Kids" in the speciality section with my friend, Roma Cafolla. Her mother, my first music teacher, was accompanying us, but just before the day she fell ill and we had to withdraw. As I had already paid the £1 subscription, Father Daly, the organiser, encouraged me to enter for the folk section accompanying myself on my guitar – even though I insisted I could only strum a few chords and croon away to songs like "Plaisir d'Amour" and "House of the Rising Sun". Still, I felt I had nothing to lose, and to my amazement I actually came second.

That gave me a little confidence, and I put a bit more time into practising my singing and guitar playing. A few weeks later, there was another contest so I had another go at a three chord wonder, and nobody could have been more surprised than me when I won first prize. Through this I was introduced to Tony Johnston. Tony was headmaster of Mullabuoy Primary School, six miles from Derry. He spent his spare time teaching and promoting promising young singers. At that time, his big hit was a girl called Majella Brady whose fame as a pop singer was spreading even beyond Ireland. When he suggested taking me under his wing, I don't think Tony glimpsed in me anything approaching Majella's talent, so in the months ahead I was occupied mainly with accompanying Majella on the piano.

But the most important thing to take into consideration was my O-levels. The exams were just coming up so Tony struck a bargain with my dubious parents, arranging that he would coach me on the academic side at the same time as helping with my singing career. He was a fine teacher and for the next few months my nose was firmly glued to the grindstone, but it paid off as I emerged, stunned and exhausted, with seven good O-levels.

With my O-levels behind me, I decided to set my sights on getting my A-levels in Music and English with a view to training afterwards as a music and drama teacher. That seemed a more practical and versatile option than teaching ballet, and, anyway, everyone thought it was sensible to get trained for a "proper" job and not base too much on the dubious prospects of singing. Most of my friends were planning to go to college or university, and although I enjoyed my singing, I couldn't honestly see myself ever making a living by it. I still got too nervous about performing to want to do it full-time, and besides, I wanted the security of a steady job, and the opportunity of staying near my family and friends.

Only my friend Aileen and I took A-level music, and in the

unaccustomed freedom of the sixth form we spent hours in the practice rooms, playing the piano, with Aileen stopping every now and then to fish yoghourt and fruit from our secret store under the piano lid.

Yet almost despite myself, my singing career was looking up. Tony had sent a tape of me singing songs we'd written to Michael Geoghegan, the manager of Rex Records in Dublin. He liked my singing and gave me a recording contract. My first single was a song written by Tony called "Sixteen", with a song I had written myself, "Little Girl Blue", on the B side. The record wasn't a phenomenal success – in fact, it was a dismal flop! – but it got me several openings in local TV and radio, and paved the way for more discs on that label.

Actually, making that first disc was a wonderful experience. I hadn't any idea how records were made or what a studio looked like. Then there was the thrill of singing with a big band for the first time. I put everything I'd got into my up-tempo track, jigging and bopping around until after the seventh take I was absolutely exhausted. I remember crawling outside afterwards and sitting on a wall in a daze until my head stopped reeling, thinking I'd never do that again! A certain amount of publicity went with the release, and on the morning it came out, I stood at the bus stop outside the newsagent's, straining my eyes to take furtive glances at the girl in the red dress with the guitar on the front of the paper, yet afraid to let anyone see me looking at it too closely! It didn't give me any jumped-up ideas that I was a big star, but I did feel a sense of pride and achievement.

I was also beginning to appear more in cabaret and folk clubs. Sometimes these were just poky little rooms filled with smoke and I would come on for a few minutes near the end of the show. As soon as I was finished I'd have to get outside as quickly as possible and take deep gulps of fresh air. Even to this day I can't stand smoky rooms. Still, looking back it was a very valuable training ground and apart from the occasional lack of oxygen there were some very happy memories – like the time when I was crowned Queen of Cabaret at Clontarf

Castle in Dublin, one of the main clubs in Ireland. I had sung several times there, and at Liberty Hall, another famous place, and I was overwhelmed by the appreciation and support which lay behind this honour. On Easter Saturday 1968 I was dressed in a beautiful evening gown, and seated like royalty in a majestic white Rolls-Royce. Then the motorcade moved off slowly through the cheering crowds as the Finton Laylor Band piped us through the packed streets to the Castle. There, after a speech or two, and an exuberant burst of trumpets from the band, I was led in a daze to the throne in the centre of the stage, and found a glittering tiara being placed on my head. I felt like Miss World, but I told myself to stop being so ridiculous. I was plain Rosemary Brown.

Well, to be accurate, by this time I was called Dana, as Rosemary Brown was considered a bit long and cumbersome. I didn't exactly like the thought of changing my name and I was anxious to make the right choice so I took a list of names in to school, and asked my friends to choose. One of the possibilities was "Marie St Colm Cille" from the Gaelic name for Derry: Doire Colm Cille. Colm Cille means "the dove of the Church" and Doire means "the oak grove". There were hundreds of these trees scattered all over the city and surrounding area. Not surprisingly, it didn't get many votes – which is probably just as well as I'm not sure how to spell it even now, and can you imagine trying to sign autographs with a name that long!

It was "Dana" which was the out-and-out favourite. Dana is an old Gaelic word meaning "bold" or "mischievous", and as Eileen had become quite a judo expert, I had developed a reputation for toughness in defending myself from her attacks – and in trying out some of her tricks on unsuspecting friends. Dana was also the queen of an ancient Ulster tribe which had been dedicated to poetry, music and dance though I didn't learn this until a few years ago. All in all that was the name that seemed to fit the bill best.

Michael Geoghegan was there that day at Clontarf Castle. He was fast becoming an invaluable friend, and over the coming months I recorded four more numbers with Rex Records. Then I was asked by the RTE (Irish television) producer Adrian Cronin to appear in Ireland's top TV programme, *The Late, Late Show.* It was terrifying to be performing in front of an invisible audience of thousands for the first time, but it all went smoothly, and Mr Cronin and Gay Byrne were very understanding about my shaking legs and scarlet cheeks!

On the recording side, my repertoire ranged from original material by Tony and myself in both media, through Joan Baez, the Seekers, and my idol, Cliff Richard. I also sang Irish folk tunes. Everyone had their own opinion as to which singer I sounded like, but for some reason everyone seemed to think there was something quite different and special about my performance. After I won a talent competition once, the adjudicator, the late Phil Donohue, remarked that it had been my presentation which had impressed him most. People said I had a way of holding a crowd.

Personally, I couldn't understand what all the fuss was about. I certainly wasn't modelling myself on anyone; I was just myself. In fact, when people asked me who I wanted to be like when I grew up, I used to say, "Rosemary Brown." So perhaps part of this mysterious "ingredient X" was simply that I wasn't at all enchanted with the world of show business, and as time went on, I became more and more sure I didn't want to devote my life to it. My nervousness never improved, and if anything the stomach cramps and shaking knees got worse under the pressure of increased engagements. I never seemed to develop that shell of cool sophistication which other performers possessed. Still, maybe that actually helped my stage image, as it made people rave about the young Derry girl's simplicity and freshness. I was just scared stiff! And completely naive. On the other hand, I never lost my love of the music itself, and once I'd got into the song I could often forget about the butterflies in my stomach and just get lost in the beauty of the words and melody.

In the winter of 1969, after I had been with Rex Records

for about two years, the secretary of the company asked me to enter for the Irish National Song Contest whose winner would go on to represent Ireland in the Eurovision Song Contest. With mixed feelings I agreed to do it, and was chosen to sing a song called "Look Around", by a well-known writer, Michael Reade. The dreaded night in February came, and the show was to be broadcast live on RTE.

It was the first time in my life I experienced real terror! The programme was to start with a medley of songs sung by all eight contestants, and my heart was thumping like a pneumatic drill in my ears as I waited for my turn, gazing at the studio door like a petrified rabbit cornered by a stoat. Suddenly my eye was caught by a strange movement by my side, and I noticed another competitor, Butch Moore, agitatedly rubbing his hand on his thigh in obvious panic. I felt a rush of sympathy for him, and was slightly encouraged that I wasn't the only person feeling we were awaiting execution. I was so absorbed by Butch's agonised plucking at his trouser leg that I hardly realised it was my turn to sing. Before I had time to faint or scream, I found myself on the stage and fighting my way through the first bars of the song. With that hurdle over, we went on to sing in the contest proper, and somehow, still shaking with nerves, I managed to get through it without any obvious bloomers. Then it was just a question of sitting back and waiting while the judges came to their decision. It was a close competition with performances that seemed so polished and assured that I couldn't see how I could possibly win. But just for good measure I actually prayed that I wouldn't. The scores were announced, and to my joy I found that I had been placed second. My family were delighted that I'd done so well, Tony was philosophical, and I was secretly thanking God for saving me from a nervous breakdown.

During the spring and summer of 1969, I felt much more contented. I had come to an important decision about my life. As a performer, I was just too insecure. It had been fine singing harmony with my sisters, but, with the exception of feises where I felt at home, I didn't have the confidence to make a solo artiste. Tony Johnston was very understanding and I think my parents were privately quite relieved that I was going to settle down to a more normal teenager's life and spend a little more time with my own family. My sole ambition now was to become a music and drama teacher, and apart from just a few singing dates in the summer, I spent most of my spare time teaching piano and guitar to a few youngsters from Tony's school which brought in some useful shillings. I really enjoyed my academic study at last, and was almost looking forward to the A-levels the following summer.

In addition, far more important things than singing were going on around me. In 1967 we had moved from the Creggan down into the centre of Derry, to the fifth floor of a new block of flats in Rossville Street (later to be known as the Bogside) near where my mother had been born and brought up. My grandmother had moved there too. Dad had opened a barber's shop on the ground floor, and Robert and Eileen worked alongside him, Eileen doing the women's hair at the back of the shop. Everything in my world seemed bright and secure at last, but it was a very different picture in the city.

For some time now I'd heard the people talk of how Derry was declining. The docks, once so busy and prosperous, where my father and his father before him had worked, were now all but closed. I used to walk with my friends on Saturdays along the quay and it was a scene of decay and dereliction, a ghost-land. The wood on the jetties was all rotten and the huge warehouses stood dusty and silent. Industry was leaving the city. There were even fewer jobs now and Derry, the second largest city in Northern Ireland, had one in five men out of work.

I became more and more aware of how dissatisfied people were. The news was full of talk about discrimination for jobs and homes and jerrymandering of local councils. Feelings began to run high. I had never been particularly interested in politics but suddenly I found myself, like everyone else, scanning the newspapers from end to end and sitting glued to the television news as the situation became more intense.

This wasn't just theory now. It was my home and I was seeing the community being broken up.

The grievances were expressed through organisations like NICRA, the Northern Ireland Civil Rights Association, and in peaceful marches and demonstrations. Then came the fateful Civil Rights march and the Burntollet Bridge incident in 1968, and it seemed like the cap had been taken off a bottle of fizzy pop. In no time at all, petrol bombs and stones clashed with batons, water-cannons, tear gas and rubber bullets.

At first it was just unreal. We watched many riots from our flat window, and it was like seeing an awful war film. Derry had always been so quiet. My mother and her generation just couldn't believe it. In bewilderment and distress, they kept saying, "What's happening to our city?" Mum used to tell me that the assizes court hardly ever stopped in Derry because nothing serious ever went on. I'd never heard of anyone being murdered there, and it had always been quite safe to walk out alone at night in the city. I remember one particularly beautiful Christmas night just before the start of the Troubles. We'd been to Midnight Mass and the sky was crisp and clear. While our families got together to celebrate the new Christmas morning, my cousin Philip and I sneaked off and walked round the walls of the city. The night was so still and we walked in silence, never feeling frightened or threatened. That was the Derry I knew.

Now the city began to resemble a bomb site. We became afraid to go out. Even when shopping, it was quite common to get caught in a street riot and many of us did. You just had to run for cover. There were many anxious times while we waited for a member of the family to get home safely. It was not only frightening but very, very sad. Dad's shop was now all boarded up though a forlornly hopeful sign hung outside saying "OPEN". The baker's where we used to buy doughnuts on the way to school was all burnt out. Our old shoe shop was gutted. The busy shopping centre was becoming a ghost-town, too. From our flat, we could see spirals of smoke and smell the tear gas fumes. I used to think that Derry was slowly burning on her funeral pyre.

The Troubles were the topic of every conversation. My friends and I would discuss all the newspaper reports to the last detail. Now I even read the Government reports and the accounts of what had been said in Parliament. Every word was riveting. I suppose the only thing which stopped us getting into real despair was the fact that we just couldn't believe it would last. No one could. It was partly something to do with the famous Derry humour, our optimistic approach to life. There was the well-known story about the police charges at a certain barricade. Regular as clockwork came the charges, every half hour or so. Each time, the "boys", as they were called, pushed them back. Then suddenly all went quiet. The story goes that the boys were so concerned that they sent someone out to look for the police in case anything had happened to them.

But gradually it became clear that the Troubles were far from a joke. Instead of getting better, they got much, much worse. Soon we were watching truckloads of soldiers rolling into the city and hearing the sickening sound of gunfire. There were checkpoints at nearly every corner. More and more the city was disappearing in a cloud of smoke. To me it came as a great shock that people could feel such distrust and fear of each other. Even now I can't really understand it. There seems no political answer, not even any room for negotiation, when some hearts and minds are so closed. All I can say today is that we must pray that the barriers of distrust and prejudice can be broken down. At the time, though, I was utterly bewildered and deeply upset like everyone else, and I was just lucky, I suppose, in having my studies, my music and a strong, protective family to give my life some sort of stability and purpose.

5

The situation was still smouldering angrily when, at Christmas 1969, Tom McGrath, the producer of the National Song Contest, rang out of the blue and asked if I would take part in the next competition in February 1970. Although I was surprised and pleased to be asked, I'd definitely decided by this time that I didn't want a career in singing. Thinking that took all the pressure and worry out of the idea. The school agreed to let me have time off to go down to Dublin, and I quite enjoyed what I thought was my last fling before settling down to the serious business of getting my A-levels and earning a living.

I felt fairly relaxed on the actual night, and was even able to laugh at the last minute panic over my hair. The RTE girls did an elaborate style with little pigtails on the top, but when the producer saw it he was horrified. With only half an hour to go, it was too late to do anything about it except let my hair flow down naturally and put a clasp on the right side to stop it falling into my eyes. I wasn't nearly so troubled by nerves as before, and, besides, I really loved the song which had been chosen for me, "All Kinds of Everything" by Derry Lindsay and Jackie Smith. Even when I was being nearly suffocated by my ecstatic family and told that I'd won, I didn't faint at the thought of taking part in the Eurovision Song Contest, perhaps because I never thought for a second that I had a chance of winning and also I was much more worried about whether I'd get good grades in my exams. Innocence is bliss . . .

The Eurovision Song Contest was to be held in Amsterdam on March 21st, and the next few weeks passed in a rush of frenzied activity, visiting London to see Phil Coulter (of "Puppet on a String" and "Congratulations" fame) about arranging and recording the song, doing endless interviews and photographs and getting ready for the adventure of a visit to another country. I'd never been outside Ireland and the British Isles before and to tell you the truth I thought everywhere abroad was boiling hot so I was careful to look out all my pretty cotton dresses and light summer clothes.

It was just as well my nerves weren't in their usual frayed state over this competition. Just two weeks before the contest, I was being driven by Tony and his wife Eithne down to Dublin for an appointment with RTE when the car skidded, left the road and overturned. The car was a write-off, but, amazingly, the worst we had to show for it was some cuts and bruises and a certain amount of shock. But even with this, the pace didn't falter. I was beginning to understand the saying, "The show must go on!" A passing motorist gave us a lift to the Montrose studio where we arrived one and a half hours late, but in time to go ahead with the wardrobe session. Later in the evening, and after several cups of weak, sugary tea, I went on to sing at a hotel in Co. Kildare.

Four days later, I was given a civic reception at the Derry Guildhall to make sure I had a good send-off in the true home-town tradition. I was really touched by everyone's friendliness and encouragement, especially when Brian Martin, the Development Commission Chairman, presented me with a huge bouquet and made a short speech, saying something like, "We in Derry are very proud that Dana has been chosen and we feel that she will be a wonderful ambassadress for the city. We wish Dana every success and we know she will uphold the cultural and musical traditions of our city."

I felt proud, too, proud of Derry and all the benefits and blessings she had given me. I stood up and thanked them all for the honour of being able to represent them, and said that it was my greatest wish to present a brighter image of my native city to the world. It wasn't until I crawled exhausted into bed that night and caught sight of a huge pile of school-books that I remembered with a pang of guilt that I hadn't opened them for a month and my A-levels were less than three months away. I would really have to get down to work after Easter. Somehow that was a comforting thought and I was soon asleep.

That same week a Dutch film crew came over and made a short film of me to be shown during the contest. I tried not to think of the millions who would be watching it, though I was getting a bit more used to television cameras – as well as press reporters springing up in all sorts of unlikely places. I had just appeared on *The Late, Late Show* again, and I sometimes felt that Derry knew more about me and my movements than I did myself. The Bogside in particular was bubbling with excitement. People coming into Dad's shop demanded to look at press cuttings while he cut their hair. A few days before we left for Amsterdam, flags and bunting appeared all over the block of flats where we lived. The day before we flew, Mum, Granny and I were invited to the Bishop's House, and there the Bishop of Derry, the Most Reverend Dr Farren, gave me a gift of a plaque of Dürer's *Praying Hands*. I thought it was so thoughtful of him. It meant a lot to me and I still have it today.

At last our departure day arrived. After some surprising resistance from Tony, it had been agreed that Mum and Gran would come with us, along with Tony's wife and a close friend of ours, John Daley.

Early next morning we arrived at Dublin airport where we were waved into the grey sky by a small enthusiastic crowd of well-wishers (I think it was just two cleaners and a few porters!). Once in the air, I felt in my bag to make sure I'd packed my suntan lotion and glasses. After a stop in London, we touched down a few hours later amid the same grey clouds and icy rain. For a moment I wondered if we'd landed in the wrong place, but no, the captain's voice reassured us that this really was Amsterdam. I felt my holiday dreams crumbling. Getting out of the plane was like walking into a large fridge. During our first day there we were left very much to our own devices, and I remember wandering round Amsterdam feeling very cold and very lost, unable to speak a word of Dutch! Then the relief we felt when we stumbled upon a Wimpy's. There was a piece of home! We all tucked into hamburgers and chips and felt a hundred times better. But I soon discovered that there wouldn't have been a lot of time for basking in the sun anyway.

The next week was a bewildering round of functions, rehearsals and interviews, but it was made all the more exhausting by the undercurrents and tensions which were beginning to break through the surface. One problem was over what I should wear for the contest. A young Dublin designer, Maura O'Driscoll, had submitted some sketches to Tony some weeks before, and we had been so impressed with them that we asked her to make up two of the dresses. We knew at once that one of them was just right for the Eurovision Song Contest. It was a simple cream baineen mini dress, beautifully embroidered with a traditional Celtic design, which seemed to suit my personality and the song. Unfortunately RTE had other ideas. They had designed another dress for me, trimmed with Irish lace, beautiful in its way but somehow just not me. Right up to within a few days of the contest itself, there were disputes about what I was to wear, but luckily for me some of my luggage got lost between London and Amsterdam and among it was my RTE dress, so in the end I was able to wear the dress I'd fallen in love with.

Initially I wasn't aware of all the disagreements going on between the Irish team and Tony. The songwriters, Derry and Jackie, who were lovely fellas, felt they had received a pretty raw deal out of the whole occasion, and the RTE production team and other journalists were grumbling about the way they felt Tony was monopolising my time. Perhaps the root of the problem, as I look back on it now with more understanding, was that Tony was desperately worried that I would be snatched away from him by one of the big-time agents who would persuade me that I needed proper professional management if my career was to develop. I'm sure he was concerned for me too, that I might be swallowed up by the sharks, but his protectiveness gradually became like chains around me. The most distressing thing – though, again, at the time I didn't realise quite what was going on – was that he seemed to be trying to cut me off from all contact with my mother and grandmother. It wasn't until the Irish team told me that they felt Mum and Granny were being badly treated that I realised something was wrong. By this time it was nearing the end of the week. The worst thing was that because of my ignorance I hadn't protested on their behalf and it must have appeared to Mum that I just didn't care. Late as it was, I had a long talk with Mum and Granny and the Irish team. It was quite a shock to realise how high feelings were running over many incidents.

The day of the contest was drawing closer and closer and in the midst of all the glamour and the sophistication of those international stars, I shrank more and more into just a schoolgirl. Julio Iglesias was the Spanish contestant. I thought he looked like a very handsome matador. If I'd really compared myself with all those confident professional artistes, I would never have been able to cope with my nerves so I deliberately didn't go down to watch the others rehearse during the week. I felt gauche and immature, and I found that I couldn't accept compliments and that put me into a really embarrassing situation.

After one of the functions, I was stumbling off to bed when I bumped into a tall, distinguished-looking man in the foyer. Before I could creep away, mumbling apologies, he took my arm and said, "You're a very pretty girl, and you know, you've got a very good chance of winning this competition."

I couldn't believe he was serious, and thinking he was either laughing at me or trying to chat me up, I pulled away and replied with a cheeky grin, "I bet you say that to all the girls."

He laughed and let me go. Next morning, I discovered that the man I'd been so rude to was Billy Cotton Jr himself, head of BBC TV Light Entertainment. I was too ashamed to go and apologise, but thankfully he must have taken it in good heart because he related it to a dressing room full of people, after an Engelbert Humperdinck TV show some years later, and took great delight in teasing me about it.

Well, somehow I managed to get through to Saturday without causing an international incident by insulting some famous celebrity, and in fact I even managed to make a friend in England's Mary Hopkin. I met her at one of the functions and she was so lovely and friendly. I was a fan of hers anyway, so meeting her was a great thrill for me. She treated me like an equal and really seemed to take my singing seriously with encouraging advice and assurances that my song really did have a chance of winning the contest. I thought that was so generous of her as she was strongly tipped as the favourite with her beautiful, clear voice and polished performance of "Knock, knock, who's there?"

So this was it, Saturday March 21st 1970. The Eurovision Song Contest had arrived. We had had a dress rehearsal in the morning when for the first time I'd seen and heard the other contestants perform their songs – they all seemed so confident and relaxed. Throughout the day, despite my effort to prevent it, the excitement and tension of the coming event filled my stomach with a thousand butterflies so that I couldn't eat or rest. I just prayed that nerves wouldn't get the better of me and ruin everything. Now here I was sitting on some steps at the back of the stage area, playing "I spy" to take my mind off things and watching, fascinated, as Julio Iglesias whirled around in a big black cloak, practising his scales. I'd never heard anyone warming up their voice in public before and it made me feel very embarrassed for him – I kept looking around to see if anyone else was looking at him!

I was the last to sing of the dozen contestants. I had thought my wait would be an eternity, but in fact it sped by and suddenly there was the stage manager telling me to stand at the side of the stage. It was my turn. Funny, the thoughts that flashed through my mind at that moment. I could see Dad and the family watching the television set at home, and my friends and even people I didn't know. Suddenly, I got very cross with myself. I only had to sing for three minutes. I mustn't ruin it. Three minutes that meant so much to so many people. I just had to get out there and do it. Then I heard my name announced. Would I make it down the ramp without slipping? Would I manage to climb up on to the tall cylindrical stool I had to sit on? It was a bit like perching on a chimney.

Suddenly I heard the introductory music for my entrance and I found myself walking down the ramps on legs which seemed about ten feet long. As I sat on the stool and began to sing "All Kinds of Everything" I tried to shut out the swimming faces of the huge audience and let the beautiful words and melody of the song catch me in their usual magic. For a second, as the last note died away, you could have heard a pin drop in the vast auditorium. But as I slipped off the stool with an enormous sense of relief, I was almost startled by the loud applause that broke out, and I remember thinking that the Irish team must be doing a lot of hard clapping.

Backstage, it was reassuring to find myself standing next to Mary Hopkin who gave me a warm smile and stayed with me, joking and chatting, her arm around my shoulder, while the votes came in from the twelve juries. I watched the first score put up, but after that I just wanted to savour this final taste of what had been to me like a fairy tale. I gazed round at all the stars in their glittering finery, probably the last time I would see such famous people at close quarters, their faces a little strained as they watched the scoreboard, applauding each artist whose song received votes. But suddenly Mary Hopkin was congratulating me excitedly. A massive vote had just come in for me from Belgium, putting me in the lead with just one vote to go. The next moment, the stage manager appeared from nowhere and said, "Congratulations, you've won," and Mary flung her arms around my neck and gave me a big hug. The stage manager might as well have been speaking

Chinese. I just couldn't understand what he had said, but a second later the final vote was entered and it was officially confirmed that I had come first with Mary Hopkin close behind. Then I was flabbergasted.

I had never really considered that I might actually win the contest. I'd just hoped to get through without letting too many people down. But now the incredible reality hit me like a sledgehammer and the room began to swim. Seeing me looking dazed, someone handed me a glass of water which I promptly swallowed the wrong way and started gasping and spluttering till I was red in the face. I'd hardly recovered when the manager gently pushed me out on to the stage, and in a dream I found myself beside Derry and Jackie as we received our awards. Then someone started to propel me towards the stool, and as the band struck up the opening bars of "All Kinds of Everything" I remembered I had to sing the song again. I'd never sung it with such joy – or maybe it was relief. Afterwards, wild applause broke out again. But the next minute I was glued to the stool in terror. It looked as though the entire audience was making a mass attack on me.

Hundreds of people were surging on to the stage. Cameras were clicking and within seconds I was blinded by the flash-bulbs and deafened by the shouts of reporters to look this way and smile the other. Derry and Jackie were at my side giving me a big kiss, the Irish team were dancing a sort of wild jig and Tony kept clapping me energetically on the back.

I was searching the crowd for my mother and there she was. In a flash she was hugging me and for the first time I felt hot tears welling up in my eyes. I tried to push them back, telling myself not to be ridiculous. I mustn't act like a baby now. As we went off the air, the organisers just allowed the chaos to reign for a while before I was borne along by the wave of enthusiastic well-wishers and press to the grand champagne reception that had been arranged in honour of the winner. I was beginning to feel starving by this time, but I never had a chance to eat a thing. Every time I tried to stab a piece of food with my fork, someone cried, "This way, love!" or dazzled me with a blaze of flashbulbs so that I couldn't see the plate. I was excited, and thrilled for myself, my family, for Tony and all the Irish team. Everyone was laughing and toasting our win – I felt like Cinderella.

But even at this celebration party there was tension. Long before the party was over, Tony felt that I'd have to leave. This caused an outcry and consternation among the Irish contingent and my mother and grandmother felt it was ungracious for me to leave the celebrations. But Tony insisted, and amid much ill feeling we abandoned the party, with me too weary to protest.

Outside, the first thing I did was phone Dad and the rest of the family back home. He told me how proud he was and about all the wild celebrations which were going on in the Rossville Street flats and down below in the Bogside. It was hard to say goodbye.

After the phone call, I hoped I would be able to sneak away and get to bed, but I had endless interviews and was bombarded with questions until 5 a.m. when my brain finally curled up into a little ball and refused to function any longer. The reason for all the fuss was that no one knew anything about me as I'd been hidden away from the limelight all week, and there was panic amongst the media now that an unknown had walked off with the prize and none of them had any copy for the next day's papers. By the time I crept exhausted into bed, I had begun to think how much more peaceful it would be to *stay* a nobody. Again, the one comfort as I drifted into oblivion was the thought of returning home and to school on Tuesday to study for my A-levels.

Just four hours later, when the interviews started again, I began to realise that all hope of retreating into that comfortable obscurity was evaporating like the morning mist. It was as if I'd become public property. The press conference was temporarily adjourned as we escaped to Mass, but when we returned to the hotel, I was whisked off round the canals by the television crews so that they could get their films of the new "star" to display to the public back home.

In the evening there were more interviews, and about midnight I was left to start packing for the following day's flight. How I longed to be home. It was as if I was an exhibit in a cage, being viewed and inspected by curious strangers, unable to communicate with the people I needed most.

I felt so confused. My head ached with lack of sleep, the constant questions, and being shunted around like a piece of baggage. It tore me apart to think how Mum felt, and at the same time I had loyalties to Tony as well. I knew I had a whole lot of growing up to do really fast, but I couldn't see how I'd ever keep everyone happy. Still, tomorrow I would be back in Derry with my father and family. Then everything would be all right.

One ray of comfort came next morning when I was showered with telegrams from friends and well-wishers. It was like a hundred birthdays rolled into one, and sitting up in bed opening the pile of cards I felt overwhelmed by all the love they expressed. Far from feeling proud of what I'd achieved, I'd never thought of myself as such a complete failure because I could see already that it didn't matter how successful you were in public if you couldn't bring happiness to the people closest to you. But the cards and telegrams did cheer me up. They were from people from every walk of life, even one from the President of Ireland. One of the loveliest was, "You have done your city an outstanding service. Derry is proud of you." There was talk of me appearing on many important TV shows such as with David Frost and Tom Jones. It was exciting but still somehow unreal.

At last the afternoon came and time to set off for home. Aer Lingus had laid on a special Boeing 737 to take the team home with the words "OPERATION DANA – EUROVISION 1970" blazoned across its side. The flight was one of the highlights of the whole week. A superb meal had been arranged with champagne and everything on the menu called after something to do with Derry. Everyone was in high spirits, and I handed out little presents to the whole team for all their hard work – keyrings for the men, and Dutch clog brooches for the girls.

As we approached the Irish coast, the captain called me into the cabin, and I gasped with amazement when the Dublin airport came into view. As we flew over the terminal building, I could see thousands of people waving. Banners and flags welcomed me home on every side as we glided to a halt. I had a crazy desire to run and hide under one of the seats or lock myself in the loo, but somehow I managed to pull myself together, dawdling over packing my hand luggage so that I was last out of the aircraft behind the reassuring back of my mother. The cheers broke like the roar of the sea over my ears, and I found bouquets of glorious flowers thrust into my hands as I acknowledged the wonderful welcome. It seemed even more like a state visit by royalty when Dublin's dignitaries stepped forward to give the official welcome. Then we squeezed a way through the clamouring press reporters to a reception room where there were speeches and interviews for fifty minutes before starting the last leg of the journey home. Fresh cheers went up as we mounted the steps and turned to wave goodbye.

It was a short flight to Ballykelly Airport outside Derry – just long enough for me to wonder what on earth the welcome would be like in my own home city. But I couldn't have been prepared for the wildly cheering crowds which surged across the tarmac to meet the plane, nor the reception which was waiting for me in the city. Brian Morton, Chairman of Derry City Commission, extended the official welcome, but his words were soon drowned by the chants of the crowd for The Song. The Nazareth Caeli Band struck up the tune of "All Kinds of Everything" and out of the air someone produced a microphone, right there on the steps of the plane, and put it in my hands in place of the huge bouquets and baskets of fruit I was clutching as if my life depended on it. But for the first time, it all became too much for me. Halfway through the song, the lump in my throat grew so big I could hardly breathe, and I broke down and wept. Then I caught sight of my father. In seconds I was down the gangway steps and into his arms. Tears rolled down his face too as we hugged each other and the band played on with the crowd clapping and cheering. Then, gradually, the officials managed to steer us into the huge limousine which was to carry us in triumph on the fifteen mile journey to the city centre.

All along the route, thousands of people turned out to wave their flags and shout congratulations and love. It was just too amazing to be real. I'd left here just an ordinary schoolgirl and now I was hearing "Dana, Dana, we love Dana. Congratulations!" on every side. I clung on to Dad's arm. He was definitely real. Every now and then, the motorcade was actually halted as the excited crowd overflowed across the road. Even so, my heart nearly stopped beating with shock at the sight which met us as we turned into the Guildhall Square.

It was awash with a vast sea of cheering, swaying people. You couldn't see the ground. They even seemed to be hanging off the buildings which lined the square, and all around brightly coloured streamers and flags waved in the chilly evening air. Somehow our car managed to nose its way to within about twenty yards of the Guildhall steps, but the officials and troops were having no success in clearing a path for us to the door. This is it, I thought. "EUROVISION STAR CRUSHED TO DEATH IN WELCOME HOME." But suddenly the amused face of an army officer appeared through the car window.

"Sorry, miss, but there's only one thing for it. I'm afraid you'll have to climb on the car roof and we'll try and carry you in!"

The whole scene had degenerated into the sort of weird dream you have when you've eaten too much cheese late at night. I wouldn't have been surprised if it had been a white rabbit poking his head through the window. As the door of the car was forced open, I found myself being lifted bodily into the air and on to the roof. From there I was passed from shoulder to shoulder above the heads of the rolling crowd. Dad was also borne shoulder high and in a few moments we were safely deposited inside the door of the Guildhall. Mum and Granny soon joined us.

There was no escape. The hall was buzzing with hundreds more excited well-wishers, but at least the chaos seemed a little more ordered, and I realised that many of the people stepping forward to hug and shake hands with me were friends and relatives, including some nuns from Thornhill and dear Sister Imelda. Pop went the champagne corks as yet another official welcome was given by a host of awesome dignitaries, but there was nothing formal or intimidating about their manner this evening. There were broad smiles on every face, and the speeches of the Chairman of the Council and both the RC and Church of Ireland bishops were full of warmth and friendliness. From outside, we could still hear the roar of the crowds continuing their own celebrations and a couple of times I slipped out on to the balcony to wave to them, feeling ridiculously like a head of state.

After two hours, my speech was becoming distinctly slurred – not from the champagne but from total exhaustion – and my jaw was aching from so much smiling. Also, once again, I hadn't managed to grab anything to eat, and my tummy was beginning to rumble embarrassingly loudly, especially, it seemed, when I talked to the bishops, so I was relieved when my parents suggested we pressed on back home.

Once more we were carried like carcasses of meat back to the car. Before I got in, I thanked the crowd for all their kindness, and then we began to edge our way through the festive streets of Derry. It was like Christmas, and so beautiful to see the city alive with celebration and happiness instead of violence. Bonfires sparkled brightly out of the darkness and tonight the Bogside flats were decorated with bunting.

Getting into the flats was as difficult as breaking into Colditz, but eventually we managed to fight our way upstairs and found the fifth floor looking like Kew Gardens with flowers and fruit hanging everywhere. It was wonderful to be with all my closest family again, but I didn't forget my one remaining goal – to find something to eat. Mum knew my appetite of old, and in a few seconds a plate of food appeared. I fell on it like a vulture. When my hunger had been satisfied, I began to feel more sleepy than ever. It was about midnight and outside the crowd still chanted and sang. If anyone was to get any sleep that night, it was up to me to do something so I stepped out on to the verandah and said another heartfelt thankyou before singing a couple of verses of "All Kinds of Everything" which they sang with me.

That seemed to do the trick. After a few more minutes of wild cheering, the crowd began to disperse with cries of "Good night, Dana" floating up on the clear night air. I groped my way to the bedroom, feeling as if I would never be able to wake up again if ever I got to sleep. Moments later I was dead to the world.

6

Incredibly, I did open my eyes again. By nine o'clock in the morning I was on the phone to my sister, Susan, in America, whose excited voice was a joy to hear. She had heard the result with a host of Irish friends, and there had been wild festivities across the Atlantic as well.

During the morning, there were more interviews and photographs as reporters started to beat a track to our door. Throughout the week, press men poured into Derry from Europe at the rate of two or three a day. The most common question was about my future – was I going to become a professional singer, or continue my studies at school? Immediately after the contest, I had been sure I would sit my A-levels as planned and think about a career as a singer afterwards. It was becoming obvious that it would be difficult to attend school full-time, but perhaps I could be coached privately if engagements kept me away too much. What I wanted more than anything was to get the security of proper qualifications so that I would have the chance to pursue my ambition of becoming a music teacher.

But I was under a lot of pressure. Mum was very keen that I should go back to Thornhill – she had no illusions about the glamour of show business, having already received enough hurts to put her off it for good. Tony, on the other hand, quite naturally wanted to reap the benefits of all our hard work and was determined that I should seize every opportunity to become more widely known.

Money. Everyone seemed to be talking about it, calculating how much I was worth, how much I stood to make from the competition, how we could increase it by exploiting all the publicity. But it all left me cold. I really didn't care about the money. Some people said I should make £250,000 that year out of records and performances; Tony put it at nearer £500,000. But the figures were meaningless. The week before I had had just £1 to spend on myself. The only thing I wanted to do was buy my parents a house, but apart from that, I considered their peace of mind and my personal happiness as more important than anything else. Unfortunately, what I wanted didn't seem to interest people much.

On the Tuesday afternoon, just three days after the contest, I was driven to Aras an Uachtarain for a meeting with President de Valera. I was so glad to see Jackie and Derry there as I'd been sad that I had seemed to receive all the glory for winning the competition when it had been their song which had done it. We all went into the presidential apartments together, with my parents, my younger brothers John and Gerald, and my grandmother and Great-aunt Mary. I think the President looked more scared by the deputation than we did. We chatted for about twenty minutes, and he was very kind, saying how much he'd liked the winning song, and wishing us more such luck. He also insisted that Jackie and Derry be included in all the photographs so on that occasion at least, due recognition was given to their talent and achievement.

After more interviews, we escaped to a hotel in Dublin for a good meal and a brief rest before my first public performance that evening. But it wasn't that easy to hide. While I was in my room, I heard children out in the street calling my name so I leaned out of the hotel window and chatted with them for a while before singing a verse of my song.

It was 10.15 p.m. before I was called on stage, and by that time I was so exhausted that I really didn't have much idea of what was going on. I just knew that I had to give my all in that performance, and somehow I managed to throw my whole heart and strength into the songs that had been arranged for me. Afterwards I thought the ceiling would come down. I remember staring at the audience in bewilderment for a moment wondering how on earth they could be so enthusiastic over what must have been a very mediocre, unpolished performance. But whatever I thought about my abilities, everybody else seemed to be happy, and the clapping went on until I did an encore. Unbelievably, after the show, there was yet another reception with speeches and congratulations, and then I had to sit down with Tony and my parents for a long and difficult talk.

Eventually we broke off to drive back to Derry with matters very unresolved. It was 7.30 a.m. before we staggered into the flat, and two hours later before I finally got to bed. I caught sight of my white, puffy face and half closed eyes in the mirror and decided that whatever else happened, at this rate I'd never be famous for my beauty.

It was four in the afternoon when I surfaced again, feeling as if I'd been hit over the head with a mallet. But there was no let-up in the pace. Straight away I had to go over to Tony's for more discussions and we sat talking for many hours, of plans which were sweeping me further and further in a direction I wasn't sure I wanted to go. By the end of it, I was so shattered that when I got home I cast all restraint to the winds and munched my way defiantly through a whole box of chocolates Mary Hopkin had given me in Amsterdam.

Next day there were more plans to be discussed with Decca at a hotel in Derry. They wanted me to record an album over the next few weeks, and give promotional appearances in England and Europe. Then there were more press interviews, and finally more debates about the forthcoming album at Tony's house until 1 a.m. Friday brought the same pattern of discussions of schedules (where I mainly listened while other people organised my life), interviews and rehearsals. The next day was the same. And the next. I began to forget what it was like to go to bed at a normal hour, or eat meals at regular times. Often I didn't know where I would be sleeping that night. Sometimes my parents came with me, but there were always tensions between them and Tony. I missed their company very much as I did my friends and also the comfortable routine of school, the kindness of the nuns, and the security of being just another pupil. I had had to face the fact that I would never be able to do my A-levels that summer, but I was clinging to the hope that in a few months all the fuss would have died down and I could sit them in the autumn or the following year.

I felt as if I was caught up on a roundabout that was spinning faster and faster out of control. We had started to travel. On one occasion we visited three countries, Germany, Holland and England, within twenty-four hours. We did an Irish tour, then a European tour of Holland, Germany, Austria, France, Spain and Portugal. In April, "All Kinds of Everything" reached No. 1 in the British pop charts, and I flew to London for a pre-recording of *Top of the Pops*, but apart from that and a couple of stints in North of England clubs, I worked mainly in Ireland and on the continent, doing some live performances which were sell-outs, and a bit of TV work.

People talked about the huge sums of money I was making, as much as £700 for a performance, and estimated the vast amount I must be getting from "All Kinds of Everything" which had sold 250,000 copies by the end of April when Decca backed it up with an album of twelve songs. But I felt too exhausted and confused to take any notice. I just wasn't interested in buying loads of new clothes, I had no inclination to go out in the evenings, even if there'd been time, and holidays were out of the question. I was satisfied that it looked as though my parents would be able to achieve their dream of owning their own home and live in a small detached house a little further from the centre. I left all the financial side of things to Tony. For myself, the strain of all the travelling combined with all the tension and bad feelings had left me physically and emotionally drained, and my self-confidence was grovelling around in my boots. I saw myself as just a tin-pot little folk-singer, and all the talk of being a big pop star simply made me feel inadequate and inferior. It all seemed such a farce. When audiences used to clap and shout for more after a performance, I felt they were just being sarcastic, and I used to slouch back on stage and sing another of my pathetic little tunes, cringing as I waited for the shouts to turn to jeers. I couldn't bear meeting people and used to hide in doorways to avoid being seen, even by people I liked. I just didn't know whom I could trust any more, and I felt totally alone – and very frightened. Especially when I began to hear bells ringing in my head and voices laughing when I went to bed at night. Looking back now, I suppose I must have been on the verge of a nervous breakdown, but at the time I just thought I was going mad. I didn't know who to turn to. I hardly saw my parents, and even if I'd had the chance, I couldn't have burdened them with more worries when they were already so upset.

The crisis came at the end of May. Tony had insisted on resigning from his teaching job to devote himself full-time to my management. On this occasion, as so often, I was staying the night at Tony's house before flying to Portugal the next day. Tony didn't want my dad to come, but as my passport was at home I was meant to go there in the morning, pick it up, and just leave them all behind. I felt trapped. I had a bed in the same room as Tony's two girls but it was impossible to sleep. It was terrible thinking how hurt and rejected my parents must feel when I turned my back on them the next day, and walked out of the door alone and how upset Tony would be if I didn't. My head ached and ached with churning it all over in my mind. By three o'clock in the morning, I decided I just couldn't face seeing them, I couldn't go on being pulled in two. I would run away. It was a mad scheme but I was past thinking clearly. I just knew I had to get away to try and find myself, to find something that would make my life worth living again.

It was a black, starless night. The air struck icy cold as I slid out of bed, shivering, and pulled on my jeans and two anoraks. Then I crept downstairs, holding my breath as I went past Tony and Eithne's room, and out into a fine, clinging drizzle. The house was in the middle of the country, up a small lane about a mile and a half from the main road. To avoid being seen, I set off down another bumpy track, stumbling and tripping in the chilly blackness. I'm a terrible coward, and it took all the courage I had to force myself on through the unfriendly countryside, freezing in terror when I heard the hollow cough of a cow. After groping my way along the hedgerow for about two miles, I eventually reached the main road. For a moment my mind went blank. Where could I go now? Through the numbness in my brain, I could think of only one person I could trust. Ronnie. Ronnie, my first boy-friend who had always remained such a staunch friend, and who represented to me on that lonely road all the security and happiness I felt I'd lost for ever. Forgetting the risks, I set out along the main road towards Derry, noticing the first streaks of light appearing in the east. I started to hitch and a few minutes later a man on his way home from nightshift stopped and offered me a lift. From the way he stared at me, I suspected he guessed who I was, but something made him not ask questions.

Before long he dropped me right at the foot of the road where Ronnie lived. It was just 5.30 a.m. But Ronnie was a milkman and I expected that he would be up already, preparing for his round. A plan was beginning to form in my mind. I would ask Ronnie to take me to Belfast. I had one or two friends there working or at college, and maybe one of them could put me up while I sorted myself out and found a job.

Heart thumping loudly, I knocked nervously on the front door. To my horror, it was his mother who opened it in her dressing gown. Scarlet in the face, I stammered my apologies, mumbling that I had thought Ronnie would be up for his milk round, and that I was so sorry to disturb them. Without blinking an eyelid, she ushered me into the house, explaining that this was the one morning Ronnie didn't have to start his round early so he had a lie-in until 7.30 a.m., but that I mustn't worry as he'd be delighted to see me. You'd think I'd called simply for a cup of afternoon tea, she seemed so welcoming and unconcerned. No one asked any questions, and when Ronnie appeared, he was all smiles. While his mother went to fix breakfast, I asked in a shaky voice if he'd mind taking me to Belfast.

"Sure," he replied, looking carefully at my red eyes, "if you'll just hang on until I've done my milk round. But only on one condition," he grinned suddenly, "that you help me get through this breakfast!" I didn't need telling twice. Depressed as I was, I felt I could have eaten a horse, even two. Life was somehow beginning to seem a little less desperate.

The next three hours were my happiest since Eurovision. The milk round took us all through the area where my old school was, and we felt like a couple of kids playing truant as I hid, giggling, in the bottom of the float when I spotted a face I knew. We were chatting and laughing as if we'd never been apart. Ronnie never probed into what I was doing. But as we drove back through the town, he began to tell me a story. We had always been great fans of Cliff Richard, but one tale I'd never heard was that when Cliff was just starting out on his career, he had wanted to run away because the pressures were too much. With eyes as big as saucers, I listened in amazement as he described a situation which might have been mine.

"But what did he *do*?" I demanded, and Ronnie turned to look at me, his face serious but gentle and kind.

"He stayed and faced the music."

There was silence. I gulped and stared at the road in front. I couldn't bear the thought of going on being so unhappy. But I knew now that I couldn't run away from the situation. I had to try and save something out of the mess I was in without causing anyone else more pain. And right then the most important thing was to sort things out with Mum and Dad.

Without another word, Ronnie drove me to the flats and took me upstairs. At our door he gave my arm a comforting squeeze, then turned to go, leaving me vowing I would never forget his kindness and patience. Inside the flat, chaos reigned.

Apparently Tony had contacted my parents to say I had disappeared and they were out with the police searching for me. Eileen was in floods of tears and in seconds I was weeping beside her. But she soon pulled herself together and began to take charge of the situation. Between sobs, I tried to explain what I'd been going through, and grasping me firmly by the shoulders, she said with decision, "Well, you certainly can't go on like this. You're just not going to cope. Come on, we've got to go and talk this out once and for all with Tony Johnston."

Within minutes she had told the police I was safe, and had got round my uncle Jim to drive us out to Tony's house as my parents might have been ages still looking for me. My legs were weak as water when we walked through Tony's door, and the sight of Tony with all his family would have had me making for the car again if Eileen's arm hadn't been holding me tight. I couldn't have said anything even if I'd wanted to, my mind felt so numb, so it was Eileen who explained that I couldn't take the emotional stress of the past few months any longer and I would have to leave Tony.

A terrible row erupted. Accusations and recriminations flew through the air. And I stood there like an onlooker, too dazed and shocked to believe it was really happening. I struggled frantically to make my mind work again. I had become so mentally exhausted in recent weeks that I'd found it almost impossible to make decisions. But I felt that somehow I had to find the strength to make a clean break or my relationship with my family and any chance of happiness would be lost for ever. Uncle Jim, a quiet and strong man of few words, finally turned to me and asked simply, "Do you want to go or do you want to stay?" Choking back the tears, I murmured, "I want to go home," and stumbled past Tony out of the door.

The press and the general public gave me a hard time. I received abusive phone calls and insulting letters from people calling me an ungrateful little hussy. The impression most people got was that Tony had sacrificed everything to a scheming, selfish, money-grabbing upstart, as if I'd planned the whole split. However Tony played an important role in my life for which I will always be grateful. I am just sorry that in the end things turned out as they did.

The effect of all this bad publicity on my career was the thing which bothered me least. At that moment I never wanted to sing again. Exhausted and withdrawn, I gradually ceased to care what anyone thought of me. The BBC gave me an interview on *World at One* but I was too upset about the situation to explain how things had really been. All I stressed was that the split had been a moral and personal decision, not a business one. But I don't think many people believed me, and until writing this book I have never tried to give a public explanation of what really happened. I suppose for a long time I found it too painful to talk about. Besides, I didn't think anyone would understand.

Michael Geoghegan, the manager of Rex Records, was a great support. He phoned me straight away to encourage me not to give up singing and promised help if my parents would like me to continue with my career. They didn't know what to do. I was committed to dates and I had to fulfil them. What was more, to throw it all in now seemed like admitting defeat before we had given it a fair chance, and Michael felt that if I had the right management my singing could bring us all a lot of happiness and fulfilment. On the other hand, I was in such a state of mental and physical exhaustion that they weren't sure if I could possibly cope with the pressures of professional work. In the end, we decided to give it one last try. Michael wrote out a list of London agents and managers from a sort of *Who's Who* of show business, and urged us to go over and meet them all. If someone had offered me a trip to the moon, I couldn't have felt enthusiastic about it. But at least I wasn't going to feel alone any more. Like a sort of zombie, I packed my things, and set off for London with Mum to do the rounds.

Some of the people we visited were big names, but I was so clueless about show business that I just stared at them as if they'd come from outer space. I'm afraid I might have offended several good people by appearing bored and off-hand. I was just too tired to take much interest. There was Evie Taylor, for instance. She handled Sandie Shaw and Adam Faith, and we liked her openness and honesty. Then there was Michael Grade, and here I really did make a bloomer. I didn't know who he was from Adam. When we were ushered into his office, he noticed my sullen face and said cheerfully, "Can't you give us a little smile then!" I was so depressed and battered that all I could do was stare at him blankly, so he hastily moved on, and handed me a list of all the stars he dealt with, really famous names. Glancing through them though, it seemed to me that they were all old enough to be my parents. But in a desperate attempt to get into the conversation I ventured bleakly, "Haven't you got any *modern* stars?" The interview came to an abrupt close. He was very gracious, but looking back, I was lucky he didn't throw me out. Both feet in it again.

The agent we had put at the bottom of the list was a man called Dick Katz. He handled entirely girls, people like Mary Hopkin, Julie Felix, Dusty Springfield, Lulu, the Three Degrees, so we felt he probably wouldn't have any more openings for a female singer. But we went to see him anyway, and there was an instant rapport. Mum liked him instinctively, and even I managed a flicker of animation at his warmth and efficiency. We signed with him the next day, the first step on a long, slow haul to recovery. Soon afterwards Dad left his job so that he could travel with me all the time, and sometimes my mother came too. By this time, the family had moved out of the bomb-torn Bogside area into our new house in Duncreggan Road. Piece by piece, we began to pick up the shattered fragments of our lives.

7

My first real work in England was an appearance with Joe Loss and his orchestra at the Hammersmith Palais. Tony Johnston had refused to give me back my music so I turned up looking a real lemon with no scores for the musicians. But everyone was so kind. A cousin of Michael Geoghegan came along as pianist and helped me to write out the chords for the band who rose beautifully to the occasion and busked along with great enjoyment. The trumpets had a field day. All the same, it was an effort to push myself on to the stage that night. I felt as wooden as a garden rake and I was quite startled when applause broke out after my performance.

A couple of months later, I appeared at Batley Variety Club in Yorkshire, one of the most famous nightclubs in the country after Talk of the Town in London. It had been opened in a working class area and the managers were determined to bring in the cream of show business. Louis Armstrong had been one of the first performers to appear there so I felt pretty scared at the thought of following on from him. At the Ivor Novello Awards later that year, I was billed alongside really big stars like Dusty Springfield and Sandie Shaw. As I walked into rehearsals that day with my father, we passed a glass case advertising the names of all the artistes appearing in the show. A young couple was scanning the bill, and as we walked by, I heard the girl say, "Well, I couldn't stand listening to Dana all night!" I felt in complete agreement. I knew I was so naive, particularly when I caught my first glimpse of the hippy pop-culture as I watched David Bowie go up to receive his award, resplendent in jeans and long blond hair. Because of my father travelling everywhere with me, I suppose I had been sheltered from the drugs, sex and double-dealing which are so publicised in show business. Dad wasn't the bodyguard type, in fact he was very friendly and open, the sort of man other men trust and like instinctively, but he was very protective and seemed to understand just how insecure I felt in the middle of the glitter of the pop world. After Eurovision, I was suddenly not a person but a pop star, and that had brought its own crisis of identity. What should a pop star wear? What car should a pop star drive? Where should a pop star stay and live? People seem to imagine that when you become famous, you suddenly become a higher being, that you stop having ordinary, normal desires, and start living according to a superior list of rules and standards. I felt the pressure of being expected to conform to a pop star image, but in my heart I couldn't see the point of changing the way I'd always dressed and behaved. (I still drink Perrier rather than champagne!) Yet I did want to be accepted in the circles I had to move in now, or, at least, not to look too much like a fish out of water, and for a while I was confused as to who was really me. That's when you need your family so much, to tell you just how ordinary you are. And God – to remind you of just how small you are.

In August, though, a totally new venture came up. I had been offered the small part of a tinker girl in a children's adventure film called *The Flight of the Doves* produced by Ralph Nelson of *Soldier Blue* fame, and starring Ron Moody, Dorothy McGuire, and Jack Wild. The film was being shot mostly in Ireland, and the bit I was in was set in the ruins of an old monastery near Athlone. Hordes of people turned out to look at us, and this, combined with my sense of inadequacy in the presence of so many famous, talented actors, reduced me to a mass of jelly.

My first meeting with Ron Moody was equally memorable – but in a completely different way. I caught sight of him at a distance looking like a distinguished English aristocrat, tall and slim, in an open-necked shirt, cravat and blazer. As he drew nearer, my eyes nearly popped out of my head for I could see that he was fully made up like a woman, with rouge, false eyelashes – and smoking a pipe! Everyone was carrying on as if there was nothing unusual in his appearance at all and I decided that I had certainly lived a very sheltered life if this was quite normal in the film world. Then a few minutes later, I overheard someone describing Ron Moody's part in the film – Master of Disguises! This was his role as a lady reporter. I told him about my first impression of him many years later and we had a good laugh about it.

But I must have looked a pretty odd sight myself. Dressed in a ragged old cardigan (which I was told once belonged to Eamonn Andrews), I had to have my hair plastered with grease and my skin streaked with dirt to kit me out for my part as a tinker girl. One night I returned to the hotel complete with costume and dirty face, and got locked out by the night porter who went back to the receptionist grumbling about "them beggars"!

Despite the fascinating experience of working with such wonderful people, it wasn't much fun being made to look as ugly and dirty as possible each day so that I had to spend hours scrubbing my face and washing my hair before I could go to bed. Not my idea of a glamorous film star. And to make matters worse, it rained continuously every day. Then, soon after we had begun filming, I started to feel really unwell with awful stomach pains and a blinding headache, but I thought it was just tiredness and nerves so I didn't bother to mention it to anyone. Then, a couple of days later, I nearly collapsed on the set. After packing me off to bed, they found I had a raging fever. A liver virus was diagnosed. Luckily my sister Susan, now a trained nurse, was over from America so she came to look after me during that dismal time. The only good point was that I lost over a stone in just one week. Unfortunately, I had managed to infect thirteen other members of the crew with the virus before I took to my bed so filming was abandoned for a week while everyone nursed their ills and gazed dejectedly at the monotonous rain. Eventually the film was finished, a beautifully imaginative and colourful film with a Disney-type plot. It never became a huge box-office success, but it was a really worthwhile experience and it's regularly shown on television in many countries. I've even seen it on Canadian TV.

Immediately after my film debut, I was bridesmaid at my sister Eileen's wedding to Peter Bradley. I remember the night before the ceremony. We sat up chatting together and eating hot buttered toast till the wee small hours. Mind you, I could afford to now that I was a stone lighter!

There was a certain amount of encouragement for my singing career in September when I received a gold disc for the sales of "All Kinds of Everything". That caused a lot of excitement in Ireland as it was the first gold disc for Rex Records too. We followed it up with a new single called "I Will Follow You". This was a new departure in style for me, getting away from the sweet folk-type numbers to have something more mature and upbeat. But it never made much of an impression on the aggressive pop market in Britain. In fact, frankly it was a complete flop. But I think probably that was good for me. I had to face up to the fact that if I didn't start fighting, I was just going to be a flash-in-the-pan, a has-been at the age of nineteen. A flicker of determination began to stir inside me, and slowly I started to wriggle out from under the blanket of apathy that had been smothering me.

Meanwhile I was still tearing round the continent like a demented flea, with appearances in Holland, Luxembourg, Belgium and Germany over the following few months. The European audiences were very enthusiastic about my performance, but I knew I had a lot of work to do before I could get my act together. In fact, I had no stage act at all, and a lot of the time I just used to accompany myself on the guitar. That meant I was always sitting down, and as I'd won Eurovision sitting on a stool, people began to wonder if there was something wrong with my legs. In Germany, one viewer wrote to the TV producer to ask if I was a cripple! Just to prove that I was quite sound, he asked me if I would stand for the next show. In the months to come, producers gradually began to discover that not only could I walk, but I could dance as well. At the beginning though I felt like a carthorse and just stayed rooted to the spot, as I'd always had the steps choreographed for me in ballet. I had no confidence to move freely, and I'd got hopelessly unfit anyway, so it wasn't until 1973 at the Knokke TV Festival that I sorted out a proper dance routine and stopped looking like a plum pudding on the stage.

On one occasion in Holland, I felt completely out of my depth when I discovered that the venue for the concert I was to sing at was an open-air marquee, and all the artistes were expected to change in one small tent. Looking out on the audience as I waited for my turn, I thought they looked a fairly wild crew, and then as the music roared out over the loudspeakers, I realised there must have been a terrible mistake in the booking. This was obviously a rock festival, and most of the crowd looked high on drugs. I went into total panic. But frantic discussions with the producer had no effect. I was billed and I had to appear. Feeling as if I was about to be shot, I walked out on to the stage, horribly conscious of my hair all squeaky clean, and my neat little mini-dress. Thousands of disbelieving faces stared at me as if I'd dropped out of the sky. In despair, I launched into my first song waiting for the rotten eggs to start flying, but to my amazement, once they had got over the initial shock, they sat back with not unfriendly smiles and almost seemed to enjoy it. At the end of my performance, they clapped long and hard. I crept off the stage feeling so thankful for the kind hearts underneath the leather and hair.

I was still very shy of other stars. Everyone seemed older and more confident and experienced. Showbiz parties scared me stiff, and my brain always seemed to turn to lead just when I wanted to appear witty and intelligent. My stomach dropped into my boots when I happened to meet Cliff Richard in a corridor during the New Musical Express Awards. It took me a moment to get over the shock of seeing my idol with a beard, but when he spoke he left me dumbfounded. "Hi there, Dana! Hey, I forgive you for beating Mary Hopkin in the Eurovision!" And on he sailed. I immediately felt so guilty for doing it that I blushed scarlet and stared at his retreating back with shame. The beginning and end of a beautiful friendship, I thought miserably. But I'm glad to say it was just the beginning.

During a week's cabaret at the famous Tago Mago Club in Majorca, I was walking past the hotel swimming pool when I saw four guys who looked very familiar – though you never can tell when a person is half naked in beach gear! On the way back, I had a longer look, and my heart missed a beat. There was no mistaking them. It was the Shadows! I longed to go up and say hello but as usual I just couldn't think of a word to say. Perhaps I would just happen to bump into them if I took a dip one day, I thought hopefully, determining to go out straight away and buy a bathing costume. But I'd missed my chance again. They left the hotel that day.

One thing which stood me in good stead in the early days was the fact that I had been brought up surrounded by musicians, and there was no group of people I felt so relaxed with. So when it came to rehearsing the backing with each successive band, I found we were on the same wavelength straight away as I could understand the musical terms used. It really is like a language all of its own, and it often causes great insecurity to the singer and irritation to the musicians when one doesn't understand what the other is saying.

During the autumn, I did big concerts at the National Stadium in Dublin, the Guildhall in Derry, and at the Royal Albert Hall in London, but most of my time was spent on the continent so that I had only the odd day or weekend with my family in Derry. We had a family joke that my suitcase never got beyond the foot of the staircase. In fact, it wasn't a joke. It was the truth. It was hard being away from them so much, but I suppose it was another factor which forced me to pull myself together and grow up very quickly. When I was at home it was so good just to laugh and mess around with my brothers as if nothing had changed – but a lot of our time was spent fighting our way through the huge pile of fan mail which poured through the letterbox each day. I did like to answer as many as I could personally (and I still do), though just occasionally I had a letter which was impossible to reply to.

One of the highlights of that year was my first pantomime. I was asked to be Cinderella in a touring production opening at the Gaumont Theatre, Doncaster. Although I started off in rags again, just like in *The Flight of the Doves*, at least this time I got to wear the beautiful ballgown and glittering jewels in the end. I felt just like a kid again as I put on the sparkling clothes for the first time. The colourful fantasy world of pantomime appealed to the dreamy, romantic side of my character. Now with fairy godmothers and magic spells I was back to the beautiful world of the imaginary ballerina who used to dance on my hand.

Of course it wasn't all tinsel and romance. Humour plays an essential part in pantomime, and this was my first attempt at comedy acting. I loved it. It was wonderful the way even the old slapstick humour of custard pies and "Oh yes he did, oh no he didn't" had kids (and adults) rolling in the aisles. No two shows were ever quite the same so we couldn't get bored. And working with professional comedians, you were never quite sure what was going to happen next. Sometimes you got a laugh without meaning to. On my first night, I had to give an interview between the matinee and the evening performances. Thinking I had plenty of time, and not wanting to be disturbed, I turned my tannoy off and was soon engrossed in conversation with the young reporter. Suddenly I heard my entrance music floating down the corridor and realised with panic that I'd missed my call. The curtain was meant to go up on Cinderella strolling sadly through the wood gathering sticks. Instead the audience was confronted with an empty stage and then a red-faced Cinderella charging out like an elephant from the wings. That got a laugh straight away. But in my rush, I'd forgotten my bundle of twigs, and the Fairy

Godmother's opening lines when she appeared in a puff of smoke seconds later were meant to refer to them. Luckily the Fairy Godmother was an old hand at ad libbing, and somehow we muddled through until I had to go off-stage and face the wrath of the producer. Not a good debut.

The spring was exhausting. I went on an Engelbert Humperdinck tour of Europe – Holland, Germany, Belgium, France and Austria – with just a night or so in each. In Germany I got flu but had to carry on with a photograph session even though I felt half dead. I shouldn't think those pictures won me many fans. I was lucky I was getting my sense of humour back. I needed it, especially in Austria. While we were there, we performed in a beautiful Viennese concert hall. To match the grandeur of the setting, I wore a long, tight-fitting evening dress. After my act, I was presented with a lovely bouquet of flowers and told by the stage manager to go out and do an encore. But the technicians, thinking the show was over, turned out the lights just as I was stepping on to the stage. I promptly tripped up a couple of steps and fell flat on my face. Immediately up went the lights and I was exposed to full view lying on the stage with a gaping rip right up the back of my dress. Grinning all over their faces, the band struck up "Colonel Bogey" and the audience roared with laughter. I don't know if it was my greatest disaster or my greatest success. I've had a good following in Austria ever since . . .

Sometimes I felt too tired to be aware of what country we were in. At our hotel in Austria, I staggered down to the reception desk the morning after we arrived, determined to get away for just a couple of hours and enjoy myself. "Can you tell me the way to the gondolas, please?" I asked the puzzled receptionist. "You know, the canals," I explained slowly, thinking *she* wasn't going to help the tourist industry much if she didn't know where the most famous sights were. When she still insisted that there weren't any boats or canals in the city, it dawned on me that maybe I'd got the wrong place. She must have thought I was mad asking what city we were in, but it was as I suspected. This was Vienna, not Venice.

Defeated and depressed, I trailed back to my room and went to bed.

By the summer of 1971, I had crawled out of my dark tunnel. After the failure of my second record, I was now determined to prove myself, and I put everything into my next release, "Who Put the Lights Out" by Paul Ryan. It rocketed into the Top 20 in the British charts. But far more important than the money and fame it brought me, was the boost it gave to my self-esteem. Gradually I learned to stop feeling inferior and comparing myself with other stars. Bit by bit, I began to establish my own style in singing. The new confidence I was gaining meant that I was actually beginning to enjoy my work, and it was great to be spending my first summer season at Scarborough Floral Hall with a smashing bunch of people – Frank Ifield, Peter Gordino, Bobby Bennett, Alan Randall and Jimmy Marshall. They were all golf fanatics and got on really well, ragging and baiting each other about who was the best golfer. Although I'm not a golf fan, I had to watch the British Open just to get a word in the conversation. The twelve weeks there were the happiest since Eurovision. Most of my family were there as well and it was great to have John and Gerald around to chat and laugh with, too. There were two shows a day, and I just had to give a twenty minute performance each time so it wasn't so exhausting as the Christmas run – though I still managed to get confused about exactly where we were and what we were doing. One Sunday night the whole show went over to Blackpool to do a charity performance. At the beginning of my act I started to say, "It's lovely to be here in . . ." when my mind went a complete blank. Where on earth were we? Far from being offended, though, the audience seemed to think it all part of the show, and roared back in delight, "BLACKPOOL!"

I was booked to appear the following Christmas (1971/72) in *Dick Whittington* at the Wimbledon Theatre, starring Norman Vaughan, Jack Douglas and Jess Conrad. I was playing the Mayor of London's daughter, Alice, and at the beginning of the show, the Mayor had to call me and I had to run on shouting brightly, "Here I am, Papa!" On the first night, I was ready and waiting in the wings (no repeats of last year) and when I heard my cue, I bounded on to the stage with a happy "Here I . . ." I never got any further. Half a second later, I shot off the stage like a boomerang. A nail sticking out of the flap had caught the binding of my overskirt, and I had been catapulted straight back into the wings. It was a very sheepish and embarrassed Alice who walked gingerly on to the stage a moment later.

Sadly, that panto doesn't hold such happy memories as the first. Lord Delfont was putting on the show and the night he came to see it, there was great excitement among the cast. I was determined to prove myself a shining star. But during the afternoon performance, I began to feel really sick and dizzy. Somehow I managed to stagger through the first half of the evening performance by which time I felt, and I'm sure looked, like a walking zombie. I shall always be grateful to Norman Vaughan. We had to do a duet together and not only did poor Norman sing my part as well as his own, he also had to hold me up as I swayed back and forth in front of the microphone. A doctor was called at the interval and he discovered that I had a temperature of 103°, so I was packed off home to my aunt and uncle in Romford where I spent the next two weeks in bed with an ear and throat infection. When I came back, all the other members of the cast knew each other well and I found it hard to slot in. Somehow I never really picked up the threads again, though the show itself was a great success.

I suppose after such a catalogue of disasters, things could only get better. I didn't feel that I had a great reputation to maintain so I was able just to be myself and laugh – generally – when things went wrong as I usually saw the funny side of it. It gave me much more confidence to think that no one really expected me to be glamorous and sophisticated – yet, ironically, as I settled down and began to feel more in control of my life, the press started to describe me in just that way. It amused me to see myself called cool and professional. One paper described me as a "smooth-as-silk, polished sophisticate"! But underneath, I don't think I had really changed at all, not in character at least. It was just that I felt a little more secure and self-aware. I knew myself much better, my strengths and limitations, and I was beginning to learn how to make the most of my abilities and weaknesses. The hair slide had finally hit the dust. I had much more confidence in choosing my clothes, but I've never been one to get excited about the latest fashions, rushing out to buy whatever is the new thing in the shops. If it happened to be a style I liked, that was fine, but generally I bought the clothes I felt suited me, buying just a few good quality outfits rather than lots of cheaper, trendier ones. I felt easiest in a fairly informal look (the "peasant" look was in at that time), and at home I lounged about most of the time in jeans and sweaters. On the stage and in TV studios, I was able to work out my act and learn what was required of me with none of my old panic. But my home was still with my parents, and most of my friends were still the girls I'd known at school in Derry, so with the people who meant most to me, I was just plain Rosemary. If I'd put on any airs, I'd soon have been cut down to size, but I never wanted to because as far as we were all concerned, I was just doing a job like the rest of them – except I had less holiday!

There were also people within show business itself whom I respected and who influenced me a lot. It isn't a world full of just sharks and crooks. Right from the beginning, Michael Geoghegan, the manger of Rex Records in Ireland, encouraged me enormously. He would often say in the early days, "You have to believe that *every* record you make could be a No. 1." I used to think he was mad, but now I see how wise he was in trying to shape my mental attitude for the struggle that's necessary for success and survival in show business. He has remained a good friend though he has left the record industry now. Dick Katz was a kind and honest man you could really depend on as well as being a talented agent and shrewd businessman. He and his wife, Valerie, were a tremendous support to me, and I miss him deeply since his tragically early death in 1981. I was given some good pieces of advice from others too. One was from Dorothy Squires who said, "Never resent the bad venues and the hard audiences because they're the ones that will make you a star." Another was from a one-time international singing star whose life was literally destroyed by drink and drugs. I will always remember her warning me, "Never let this happen to you." That made me determined that although I might have many troubles to face in my life, drink and drugs would not be among them.

There was another side of my life that was deeply affected by some different people I met early on. About a year after Eurovision, I was asked by producer David Winter to do a religious programme, *Sing a New Song*, for the BBC. I wasn't sure which way I was facing this time as there were such extremes in the way people treated me. On the one hand, I was being put on a pedestal as an international pop star, and, on the other, I was being treated just like a child. When I came to do this programme, I found that the people I met simply accepted me as I was, a normal human being. They were Christians with a real living faith, people who were open, honest and loving. I felt totally at ease with them right from the start. They didn't pretend I was something special, or look at me as some kind of freak, but simply talked to me as an adult and an equal. They helped me a lot in getting over my awkwardness in bringing God into my public life.

Through Peter Bye, the show's musical director, I sang in the Festival of Light in 1971 with Peter accompanying me on the piano. That was a wonderful yet terrifying experience. The Festival came about as a reaction to the infamous *Oz* magazine trials. Christians wanted to show that Jesus was alive and well and a power in the land. So a march was organised from Trafalgar Square to Hyde Park where an open-air concert was to take place. Well, 20,000 people took part in the rally, among them my mother and I. I don't know how my legs held me up when I saw the thousands of faces in front of the huge open-air platform, particularly when I spotted all the hostile *Oz* supporters pushing and shouting in the front, armed with rotten eggs. I think I must have looked so scared that they took pity on me because the heckling stopped as I stumbled through the short words of introduction to my Christian songs.

The event left a profound effect on me. There was certainly a tremendous atmosphere, with 20,000 people singing and praising God publicly, unafraid of being laughed at, and there I was in the middle of them all, singing and praising Him too, the underground and subways ringing with music. I felt a great sense of freedom but also of union with people I'd never even met before. We were the "Body of Christ" in a real way. There was such a sense of joy and well-being. I've always had a fear of being caught up in large crowds, but I felt no trace of anxiety there. Everyone was so loving and gentle with each other with lots of laughing and joking too. I could hardly believe it was really happening.

During the day I was introduced to a remarkable person called Jean Darnell, a woman with a world-wide ministry of preaching and healing. She was very gentle, yet also very discerning, and there was a sparkle, a depth of joy that made her face really shine. But she wasn't at all holier-than-thou. She had both feet firmly on the ground with a real understanding of people's problems and hurts, but she also had an unshakable belief in God's power to meet those needs. To my surprise, this busy lady drew me aside and talked to me about what she called "life in the Spirit." Although I'd always believed in the Holy Spirit, I'd never really thought about Him very much, and it seemed there was a whole dimension of power and joy which I hadn't experienced yet. She reminded me of the gifts Jesus gave His apostles through the Holy Spirit at Pentecost. They were transformed from men hiding in fear to men who were filled with a burning desire to go out and spread the message of Jesus, with power to heal and work miracles. Despite the great dangers and persecutions they faced, they were full of peace and joy. Jean Darnell explained that these gifts – wisdom, knowledge, faith, healing, miracles, prophecy, discernment, speaking in tongues, as the Bible lists them – were still available to Christians today. All I had to do was to allow the Holy Spirit to work more fully in my life. Jean talked of her *personal* relationship with God rather than just her belief in Him. I was beginning to see how being a Christian was more than something you just agreed with in your head, more even than leading a good, moral life and being kind to people. It seemed to be a question of giving my whole heart, my whole life and will to God. After we had talked and prayed together, I felt a different person. God was so real to me. I knew that He loved me, that He loved every one of us, and I wanted to tell other people about what I'd "discovered".

I left Hyde Park that night ready to put God first in everything and to pray hard for this filling with the Holy Spirit she talked about. But when I went home and told the rest of my family and friends, they were all rather sceptical, or just humoured me. Eventually I began to wonder if it had all been just an emotional flash in the pan. For some months I struggled to pray with more meaning and dedication, but without anyone to talk to and support me, I found it harder and harder to hold on to that initial joy and security I'd found. Perhaps, deep inside, I felt almost as if God had let me down, as if I'd been cheated, and soon I was so caught up with the whirl of professional engagements and the everyday pressures of living that all my good intentions gradually evaporated.

During the past two years, I had either been in hotels or staying with relatives, but eventually living out of a suitcase began to wear me out, so in 1972 I bought a house in a quiet suburb of London and moved there with my parents and John and Gerald. It brought me down to earth with a bump to have to face up to the responsibilities of a mortgage and furnishing a new house, but I enjoyed thinking about domestic things like wallpaper and curtains. At the same time, it was rather frustrating. I'd had all sorts of plans for putting the wilderness that called itself a garden into some sort of order, dreams of idly running a hoe up and down rows of tidy vegetables and gathering armfuls of beautiful flowers. But I never had a moment to shift even a stone from the heap of rubble in the garden and in the end we had to call in the experts.

It certainly made life much less exhausting being so near

central London, yet having somewhere quiet and peaceful to retreat to at the same time. When I came out of the house, I would bow first to the right towards my agent's house, then to the left to my accountant's, but once I'd closed the door behind me at the end of the day I was safe, carefully guarded by my family from any unwelcome invasion. I had all my books and belongings around me, and even my battered old piano which couldn't be tuned to pitch but was such a faithful old friend that I hadn't the heart to get rid of it. When I did get a rare free moment, I would tinkle away at one of my childhood pieces or strum on my guitar. Sometimes I'd escape from the world completely and curl up in a corner with a good historical romance.

The year 1972 was a fairly lean one for television appearances and success in the charts, but things were kept ticking over with engagements in cabaret clubs all over England, and highlights like an appearance on BBC-2's *Meanwhile* with Kenneth Williams and working with Tom Jones in a week of sell-out concerts at the London Palladium in November. I did do a series for Irish Television in Dublin that turned out to be a dismal failure. The series came in for a lot of criticism by media and public for its lack of organisation and polish, but really a lot of it was simply due to a shortage of time to plan and rehearse things. I flew into Dublin to discuss, as I thought, the theme of the series. When we landed I saw a film crew at the foot of the aircraft steps. I wondered who they were waiting for and even asked the person beside me if there was someone of importance on the plane. I knew it couldn't possibly be me as I was simply coming for business meetings. I had not a trace of make-up and my hair closely resembled a haystack.

I needn't tell you that the TV crew *was* there to meet me. Without a word to me, the producers of the series had taken the decision to set it in the 1920s, and they were filming my arrival to launch the idea to the public. That's why in the promotional film there were beautiful girls dressed in authentic 1920s clothes with lovely vintage motor cars – and yours truly in jeans, jacket, hat and sunglasses. Hardly a sight to impress the public. Ah well, you can't win them all.

All the same I really enjoyed working with the people on the programme, like Angela Vale and Fran O'Toole of the Miami Showband, a lovely talented fella who later became another tragic victim of the Troubles. During that year I also went to Madeira to sing in a festival organised by Skol, the international group of travel agents. I was only meant to stay overnight, but I loved it so much that I stayed there for two weeks and went back the following year with my mother. The stage was next to the pool down by the sea and surrounded by fairy lights. It was like another world. But in the same year, an event happened which was to be of far greater significance than any professional success. I met Damien Scallon, the man who was to become my husband.

8

Damien was a hotelier and a businessman. Our paths had crossed briefly in 1970 when a street in Hilltown was named after me and a reception was held in his hotel in nearby Newry. But it wasn't until 1972 that I really talked to him properly. Our meeting came about through a lovely mutual friend, Father Thomas, a Cistercian monk who devoted most of his time to raising money to take children out of troubled city areas into the country on holiday. A wonderful personality, soft-hearted, open and generous with a great gift in counselling and a special ministry of healing to people suffering with cancer, Father Thomas is still one of our closest friends.

With his brother Gerald and sister Josie, Damien owned the Ardmore Hotel in Newry, and offered it to me to do a charity concert in the ballroom in aid of Father Thomas's work. On July 9th, Damien came to the airport to meet my father, John and me from the plane. He was tall and handsome, with an open face and lovely green eyes (yes, you're right, he's paying me to say this). Seriously, though, I thought he was very good-looking and the kind of man you instinctively liked and trusted.

His manner was warm, but there was just a hint of shyness, so when we got into his sports car, I decided I must try and make bright conversation to break the ice. I made some basic comment about the car engine, thinking this was an area most men like to show off in, but to my surprise, he replied simply that he didn't know anything about the inside of his car, and if anything went wrong, he just stuck it in the nearest garage. I was very impressed by his honesty. I think most men would have tried to bluff to create a good impression. He must have thought I knew a bit about cars because a moment later, he demonstrated his generosity – and bravery – by asking me if I'd like to drive the sports car back to Newry – despite my protests that I wasn't a very experienced driver. (I didn't dare admit I hadn't even passed my test!) I saw Dad grow pale as I climbed into the driving seat, and I tried to look casual as I threw the car into gear and roared off down the main road. A few miles on, though, all my breezy confidence left me when I found myself trying to overtake a long queue of cars on the brow of a hill. I'd thought someone would brake to let me in, but the line was solid, and my heart began to pound as I imagined another car appearing over the top of the hill. In the back, I could hear Dad praying under his breath, but Damien sat still as a rock next to me gazing calmly out of the window as if nothing was wrong, giving me time to press my foot flat down on the accelerator and fly over the brow of the hill just in front of an oncoming car. Again, I was struck by his kindness and sensitivity, as well as by the strength of his nerve. Safe on the other side of the hill, he asked casually if I was enjoying myself and was I quite happy to drive on to Newry, but never at any stage did he mention the fact that I'd nearly killed us all. Right from the beginning, he established a picture in my mind of a man totally in control.

In fact it was a misleading impression. Damien had managed the hotel since he was twenty, and had learnt to project an image of quiet assurance combined with a great sense of humour. Damien was just himself, no arrogance or pretence, and he always appeared calm and confident, so it was only much later that I realised he was actually very shy. Friends of his told me that at times he was so lacking in self-confidence that he occasionally developed a slight stammer. But during that first meeting, he seemed relaxed and easy-going, and we got on like a house on fire. The concert was a great success. I was due to fly out the next morning but the weather turned really bad, and I was fog-bound at his hotel for several days. It was so refreshing to get away from the pressures of work and relax with someone so unaffected and kind. We also shared the same sense of humour so we quickly established an easy, light-hearted friendship.

When I eventually left, we promised to keep in touch. A few months later, I was staying in a Dublin hotel when the phone rang in my room.

"Hello there. What's the weather like with you?"

"Pretty bad," I replied, staring out of the window at the steady drizzle.

"It's not too good here either," came Damien's bland answer, "I'm just two floors up from you!"

This was typical of the surprises he springs on me. I remember one night sitting at home in London when the phone rang and it was Damien. I was surprised to hear him as he'd already rung me earlier that day from his hotel in Newry. He wanted to know what I was doing and I told him just watching television.

"Why don't you come out for dinner," he said. "I've just arrived at London Airport and I'll pick you up in half an hour."

We had lots of happy times and good laughs together.

One particular surprise hit me more like a bolt of lightning. During one of our early walks, he casually dropped into the conversation that he believed we could have a happy future together. It was a while before I could reply. The very thought frightened me. I just wasn't ready for such a huge commitment, and I knew that for me marriage was for life. What if I picked the wrong person? I think I had a childish, romantic notion that I'd know the "right man" the minute I met him. I could see that Damien had many of the qualities I would like in a husband, but nothing had told me on our first meeting that "this was the man I was to marry" – no bells ringing or voice from above. I suppose, too, I was afraid to give myself, afraid of being hurt. I could see even then that when you married, you had to make yourself vulnerable or there would be no sharing or trust, and at that time I felt Damien was so strong and independent that he would never need me, despite what people said about his lack of self-confidence.

So I tried to dismiss the idea, but to my amazement Damien actually questioned my opinion. Perhaps I'd given too many interviews where people just accepted my views without challenge. For whatever reason, I was quite shocked that he didn't simply accept what I said. We had a long discussion about the pros and cons of marriage for us. I kept saying that I didn't feel it was right for me at that time but Damien was very perceptive and said he felt I needed to deal with the real problem – my fears of any long-term relationship whether it be with him or anyone else. Maybe he was right but I didn't really know what I could do about it. In the end, we agreed to keep the friendship going and just see what happened. Over the next three years, my work kept us apart a great deal, but we kept vaguely in touch, and the bond between us deepened despite only occasional meetings. Funny little things used to happen. One Christmas, after a six month gap with no communication between us, I had my hand poised over the phone to call him when it rang and it was Damien himself calling to wish me a happy Christmas.

Life was almost too busy for romance. *Almost*, as I managed to fall in and out of what I thought was love a few times over these years – mostly ending up with a lot of heart searching and heartache. Damien was right. With him or anyone, I wasn't ready for that big commitment, or, at least, I didn't think I'd found Mr Right yet. Work-wise, though, things were looking good.

During the next year, I appeared on shows with Vince Hill, Harry Secombe, Engelbert Humperdinck and Jack Jones. A further boost to my career was winning the Best Performance Award in the International Song Festival in Lubljana, Yugoslavia, and then appearing in the show *They Sold a Million*, the BBC award-winning entry for the 1973 Knokke Festival. As well as playing Cinderella in a provincial pantomime that year, I was asked to be Maid Marian in the BBC Christmas panto of *Robin Hood.* I only had a few lines to say, and they were pretty unimaginative, so producer Peter Whitmore allowed me to change them as I liked – and that varied according to my mood! I sometimes wonder who has more fun at these shows – the kids or the cast.

In 1974, success seemed to burst like bubbles around my head. It was also one of the most exhausting years of my life, with hardly a day off, and little time for relationships – or God. It was an exhilarating feeling having everything I touched almost turn to gold; but sometimes, when I was alone, I wondered if this was all I really wanted and whether I wasn't losing sight of all the things I had held most important in life. Luckily there wasn't much time to think. After a very successful four-week Canadian tour with the London Palladium Show alongside people like Frankie Vaughan, Roy Hull and Emu, and Billy Dainty, I was asked by the BBC to do a series called *A Day with Dana.* The producer was once again Peter Whitmore, who had successes like *The Dave Allen Show*, and *The Terry and June Show* under his belt, and he had the wonderful idea of filming the series on location. I was to drive round the countryside in a sports car, arriving at destinations where I would do a concert or cabaret performance. En route I would stop at different beauty spots or places of interest and also meet up with a comedian for a comedy sketch. Everyone was very enthusiastic, and so *A Day with Dana* was born. The only problem was I still hadn't passed my driving test.

I had to learn fast. Dad was so nervous when I got behind the wheel that he could hardly bear to get in the car with me. We had a Volvo estate at that time, and it seemed to me that the car was all back to front – the handbrake was where the gearstick should have been, and I kept switching on the wipers when I wanted the indicator. Still, he persevered, brave man, and my driving test was booked for two days before the filming was due to begin. I failed.

Now we were in a real spot. Filming had already been delayed because of an industrial dispute, and we couldn't afford to lose any more time. It was meant to have been a summer show, with lots of lovely "tropical" shots, and me in light cotton dresses and T-shirts. They kept me in the light cotton dresses – but by the time we finished filming it was late September and I nearly died of cold. For one show, they had me perched like a fly high on a giant dinosaur's foot, with only a skimpy mini dress to shield me from a force ten gale. The technicians kept passing me up cups of hot tea, but my teeth were chattering so much that I could hardly drink it, let alone smile sweetly and sing my songs. It was obvious that a resourceful man like Peter Whitmore wasn't going to be put off by a little thing like my having no driving licence. He got hold of a sparkling white MG with the top rolled down, and hid the L plates where the cameras couldn't see them. Then, into the front cavity of the passenger seat, he fitted the smallest technician I've ever seen! As I was to be singing live using an earphone for the music track, we needed someone to monitor the levels and watch over the equipment, but Brian also doubled up as driving instructor, a little voice shouting out advice and encouragement from somewhere around my feet.

For the first programme, I had to drive over Chelsea Bridge, with cameras strapped to the passenger door, singing in a carefree, windblown sort of way, before driving round the square on the other side and pulling in at a mark. The hardest bit was at the beginning. I had to start off by driving down a narrow, walled, cobbled street towards the camera. I was terrified. Gripping the steering wheel as if there was no tomorrow – and there might well not have been – I put the car in gear and gently eased out the clutch, trying to smile gaily as the car kangaroo-hopped down the lane. Somehow I arrived at the bottom without scraping the car or mowing down the cameramen, and I was triumphant. Then they broke the bad news. That was just a dummy-run; now for the real take. To my amazement, I actually succeeded in reversing the car back up the tiny lane, and after that I felt I could face anything. Soon I was roaring over Chelsea Bridge with a white and petrified face staring up at me from the floor, but I was having a ball. By the time I got to the square, I thought I was

Stirling Moss. Driving was no problem after that – even though the camera crew turned pale every time I got into the car.

The series took us all round the country and into some bizarre situations. I got covered with red paint when I came upon Roy Hudd redoing a telephone box, I found Terry Scott dressed as a surgeon trying to repair his car at a garage (with passers-by swerving as they stared at him in disbelief), I acted in a silent movie with Don McLean, and went punting in medieval costume at Aylesford Castle in Maidstone. One of the most memorable incidents was when we were on location in the New Forest. I was scheduled to sing the Buffy Sainte-Marie number, "I just want to be a country girl again", and to evoke the right atmosphere it had been arranged that I would be filmed on a romantic ride through the woods on horseback.

I explained to Peter that, of course, I couldn't ride, and he reassured me that I would only have to sit on a quiet old nag and amble through the dappled sunlight singing my songs. The owner of the riding stables was asked for a docile horse, but she obviously saw this as her big opportunity to get her favourite horse on TV. Out into the yard was led a very lively two-year-old half-Arab stallion which was obviously bored out of its head. At first I was adamant that I wasn't going to get on a virtual racehorse, but the owner insisted that he had a lovely temperament and would be peaceful as a lamb. Full of misgivings, I climbed aboard – and the first thing it did was take me straight under a tree so that I was whacked on the head by a low branch. But I was still too ignorant to see the danger signals. After the dubious start he seemed to settle down to a gentle enough walk, though I didn't feel I was having much say in what direction we took. The film crew were so enthusiastic about the way this beautiful animal was coming across that they suggested a "light canter" across the field with the cameras in a Range Rover alongside. I couldn't get him to move any faster so his owner gave him a sharp slap on his rear end and before I could say "Trigger", the horse was careering off towards the distant horizon. Within seconds, my feet had come out of the stirrups, and as I ducked to avoid another tree (the animal obviously had psychopathic tendencies), the saddle slipped sideways and I was left clinging on at right angles to the horse, holding on to the mane for dear life. I was just saying my last prayers when I saw the Range Rover circling round ahead of me, and then the little sound man, Brian, standing like a domino right in the path of the bolting horse. I felt tears streaming down my face as I tried to shout, "Get out of the way, he'll kill you!" but Brian stood firm, and just as I was closing my eyes to avoid seeing him trampled under the crashing hooves, he leapt aside and caught hold of the trailing reins. The horse jolted to a halt and I was left hanging almost underneath its stomach, a gibbering, shaking wreck. The film crew winkled me off and I reeled over to Brian to thank him for saving my life. Brian was as calm as a millpond, and to my amazement simply told me to get straight back on the horse or else I'd never ride again.

I knew he was right and that the horse wasn't vicious but simply highly intelligent and very fed up with an idiot like me on its back, so somehow I pushed down the tears and sense of panic and allowed myself to be heaved on again. We still hadn't got enough shots for the film so they led us over to an enclosed area and we did some gentle walking shots.

Then Peter had another of his brainwaves. Brian was a brilliant horseman. He was also roughly the same size and build as me. Why not dress him up in my clothes and do some back shots of him galloping through the trees? In a few minutes we had got Brian dolled up in pink trousers, matching pink cardigan and a pink hairband over a long wig, which, with his hairy, bearded face, looked unbelievable. Off he went, weaving in and out among rabbit holes like Harvey Smith, watched admiringly by a family who happened to be out for a walk in the woods. Their faces, when he turned and came riding slowly back, resplendent in trouser suit and beard, were hysterical. It was the only funny moment in a fairly traumatic day.

An incident which made me realise how lucky I'd been that day happened the following Christmas when I was doing a show with Jimmy Savile. We were going round the children's wards of Stoke Mandeville Hospital, and came across a beautiful little girl called Katie whose bed was almost hidden by pictures of horses. Unable to move and surrounded by pulleys and weights, she was nevertheless so bright and cheerful that I couldn't resist going over to chat to her. To my surprise she was quite happy to talk about her accident, but I felt a sense of shock when I discovered that she had broken her back in almost exactly the same riding situation as I had experienced in the New Forest, but she was determined that one day she would be back in the saddle again. When I remembered my terror at the thought of getting on the horse again I felt really humbled by her courage and determination, and I thought a lot about little Katie in the months afterwards. In fact there was an interesting sequel to that story. In the bed next to Katie, there was a poor little girl who had just been brought in and sedated so that I didn't think she was aware of what was going on. She was paralysed and was lying asleep in such a way that I couldn't see her face. Four or five years later, I was working in cabaret when one night after the show the club manager said he had had a special request to see me from a teenager in a wheelchair. It turned out to be that little paralysed girl who had just spent a holiday with Katie and wanted to tell me that Katie now had a special saddle with a head support and was able to ride her horse to her heart's content.

The *Day with Dana* series also took us to Stoke Mandeville on one occasion, and during rehearsals many of the patients were allowed to come and watch us. Even some of the really severe cases had their beds wheeled in to see the fun from a special position at the front. The room was absolutely packed with patients and staff but for some reason my attention was caught by one particular man who was lying motionless in a bed in the far corner. I walked over to his side and asked, "Have I met you somewhere before?" To my horror, his eyes just filled with tears and he turned his face to the wall. I felt awful and although the producer then hurried me away to do the show, I just couldn't get the man off my mind. I was so sure I knew him somehow. Afterwards I asked a nurse about his strange reaction, and she explained that the man was from Derry and had told everyone how he knew my family and although I wouldn't remember him, he used to bounce me on his knee when I was a toddler. Apparently no one had believed him and so when I spoke to him, he was just overwhelmed. It struck me then, and I've realised many times since, how God can use us to bring happiness to people or meet their needs even without our realising it.

The same year, 1974, brought a most significant change in my singing career. Dick Katz felt I needed a change of direction for my recordings and that it was time to leave Decca Records so I was introduced to Dick Leahy who had just formed a new record company called GTO. It was an unlikely combination, him and me. Dick Leahy had established Bell Records in England with artistes like David Cassidy and Gary Glitter. Now on GTO records I was alongside artistes like Donna Summer, Heatwave Fox and Billy Ocean. But it turned out to be the best thing that could have happened for my singing career and heralded a new direction and quality in my recording material.

My first producer with GTO was Geoff Stevens (also a famous songwriter) and my first single was "Please Tell Him I Said Hello". I'm glad to say it went high in the charts but it took a long time to get there. When the record was first released, it did nothing sales-wise for over four months. Normally by that time a record is considered dead and you forget it and move on to something else. But two things happened to prevent that. First, Dick Leahy believed in it and wouldn't let it go. Secondly, I recorded some epilogues on Southern TV which had an unusual and unexpected effect on the record.

Let me explain that during the previous four years I continued to do the occasional Christian programme on radio and TV but not without a lot of inner struggles. To be involved in Christian work was not the "in thing" in show business. In fact, Dick Katz often pointed out to me that it could be harmful to my career – wasn't Cliff Richard suffering a lot of bad press because of his Christian views, and hadn't I already been

Islington, London, where the family came to look for work after the war. Right to left: Robert, Mr. Brown, Dana and Eileen.

Prizes from the 'feis'.

Young performers: Dana and sister Susan.

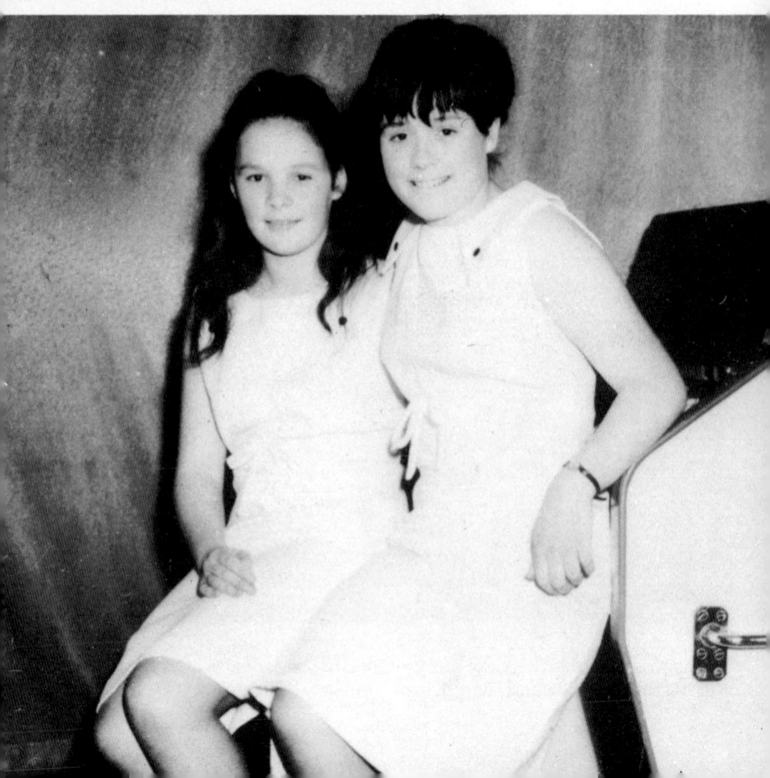

Dana with her music teacher Mother Imelda.

The President of Ireland admires the Eurovision medal with songwriters Derry Lindsay and Jackie Smith looking on.

Dana and brothers Gerald (left) and John.

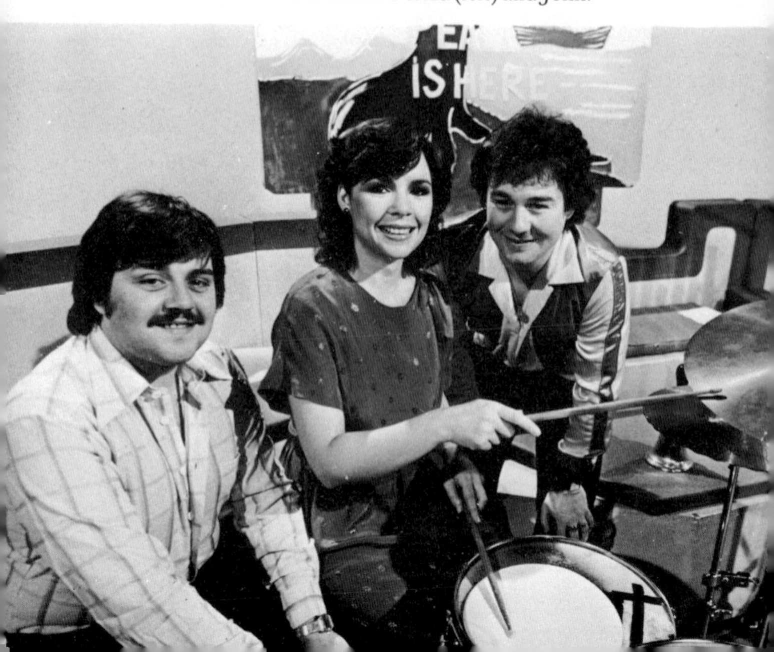

The lonely traveller.

Dana with her parents at the Irish National Song Contest.

The Girl is Back. A new image for 1979.

Like mother like daughter: Dana with Grace.

Dana and Cliff at the Royal Albert Hall.

Dana with Bishop John Taylor of Winchester and Bishop John Walker of Washington.

With Kurt Kaiser, Vice-President of music with Word Records.

As Snow White with fellow stars Les Denis and Dustin Gee.

A star line up: John Inman, Dana, Bob Hope, Jay Rufer, Des O'Connor and Grace Kennedy.

Family and friends at Ruth's christening.

Dana greeting the Pope at the Youth Rally in the New Orleans Superdome.

Dana and Damien with (from left to right) John-James, Grace and Ruth.

called "Queen of the God Slot" in a leading music magazine?

I knew all this and I had no desire to place myself in the firing line, so generally my first reaction when asked to do Christian programmes was to say no. Then the struggles would begin because my conscience didn't seem to agree. I'd ask myself, "Why did you say no? Don't you believe in God?"

To which I'd answer, "Yes, I do believe."

That was quickly followed by, "Then you're a coward."

"Yes, I'm a coward."

"You're worse than a coward, you're a hypocrite."

And so it went on. By this stage, I usually felt so annoyed that I was ringing the producer to say I'd do the programme.

Anyway, the friend in Southern TV who had asked me to do the epilogues, a Baptist minister, said it would just be a case of chatting together about my beliefs and we could record the whole programme in one afternoon. It was all quite painless and we finished recording about four o'clock. Suddenly the producer from the studio next door popped in and asked me to do a little interview for his teatime news/magazine programme which was going out live that night – and did I have anything to promote? They played a sizeable chunk of "Please Tell Him I Said Hello", and we talked about it on the programme. Thanks to that unexpected promotion, sales began to pick up and soon we had a chart hit. So the Lord does work in funny ways. It was a real lesson to me that if you obey Him, He will bless you in all sorts of unexpected ways.

That record was followed by a number of singles like "Are You Still Mad at Me", "Never Gonna Fall in Love Again", "It's Gonna Be a Cold, Cold Christmas", and "Fairytale", plus the albums "Have a Nice Day", and "Love Songs and Fairy Tales". These were boosted by dozens of TV shows, cabaret performances, theatre runs, tours and pantos.

It was a wonderful, exciting time for me – and good things were happening to people close to me too. My brothers John and Gerald had been writing songs for some time, and for one of my albums, "Have a Nice Day", the two of them wrote a couple of very popular tracks, "Goodbye Song" was by John, then a teacher of twenty-one, and "Love Me While We're Young" by Gerald, only nineteen and a carpenter. After this, John, Gerald, Dad and I established our own music publishing company called Rosey Music, and John and Gerald began working on their own LP. They were really encouraged when a song of theirs, "We Can Fly", was accepted for the Irish National Song Contest and did well. (A funny situation arose the following year when all three of us had entries as I myself had written a number for Jaimie Stone which came second.) So far they haven't been lucky enough to produce a runaway hit, but I'm sure it's only a matter of time. Gerald now has his own band and has just released a single with John which is doing very well. I'm very proud of their achievements, and both of them have been such a professional and moral support to me over the years, often working with me on TV shows and albums. With Dad as my part-time manager, too, I couldn't have been more fortunate.

Another highlight of 1974 was the making of a Christian documentary called *Who is Rosemary Brown?*. It was produced by a very fine Canadian producer called Jim Swackhammer for an English-based Christian film company called Abba. It was filmed mostly in Ireland, visiting places of importance to me, and talking about my thoughts, feelings and belief in God. This came about through my involvement with the Arts Centre Group, an organisation for Christians working in the arts, from a singer to a cameraman, a writer to a dancer. So, you see, God was still there in my life, but I hadn't attained that real personal relationship with Him. We were both just . . . hanging on to each other, I suppose. I didn't want to let Him go but I was too uncertain to want Him any closer. Too uncertain and too busy. And, of course, the busier my career got, the less time I had to keep in touch with Him.

9

I'd made it. In the world's eyes, at least, I had everything you could want – success, money, fame, good health, a stable home life, wonderful friends. Only I knew that even all these things didn't necessarily give me peace. I wasn't depressed or anything like that, but I sometimes felt worn out by the heavy physical strains of such a hectic pace. I *had* to promote records. I *had* to do television, radio, newspaper interviews and photo sessions in England, Germany, Spain – wherever they were needed. Then there were the live stage shows, cabarets, pantos, summer seasons and, of course, more recording. Everything revolved around my work. Into it went 99 per cent of my time, effort and thought. Eventually my personal life was all but squeezed out. I rarely saw my friends now but for the most part I hardly noticed. I enjoyed my work, yet it was just sometimes, particularly when I was very tired, that I would feel I was being carried along at a tremendous pace by all that was happening and that I had no control over where I was going. That was a frightening feeling. Many of my old schoolfriends were married by this time. Some had children, yet here was I, at twenty-four years of age, feeling like the eternal teenager, rushing about from here to there with hardly time to catch my breath. And so little time to think – about me, about God, about anything except WORK. But, as the saying goes, work doesn't love you when you're lonely or tired. All my security was based on material things and there were some very dark moments when I would realise how shaky my whole life was. There's a story in the Bible about a foolish man who built his house upon sand. When the storms and the floods came, everything he had was washed away. We can't avoid the storms for ever. Over the next two years I was to watch that security crumble away until there was nothing left.

The first thing that rocked me was a letter from Damien. We hadn't seen each other for ages as I had been so busy. Then suddenly he wrote to me out of the blue, a letter full of enthusiasm about a "new experience of God" he'd had, something he called "baptism in the Holy Spirit" which had brought a whole new dimension into his Christian life. He had come to know the Lord in a personal way and it had made an incredible difference to his life. He wanted to know if I realised how much God loved me and longed for me to know Him in this way. I was so staggered to hear this sort of thing from Damien, that I searched out an old letter to check the signature! Damien was a Catholic like me, and I had always looked on him as a solid, conservative type of man who would never do anything shocking or extreme, and certainly never get involved in anything remotely "fanatical". I just couldn't believe what I was reading, and I decided he must have had some sort of brainstorm. But when I saw him soon afterwards, it was obvious that he was quite sane and sober. He was full of excitement about what had happened, but I just felt threatened by it, perhaps because I'd had that feeling once and now I'd lost it. It made me feel strangely inferior and frightened so I became defensive, even downright critical. Deep down, though, I knew he had found something real and precious.

Damien was the youngest of fifteen children. His father had died tragically aged sixty-six in a motor accident in 1955 and so the eldest son Packie (Patrick) who was then thirty-five had taken over his business and the farm on which they had all been brought up. Damien's mother was a remarkable woman. A quiet strength behind her family, she held them together like a cornerstone, drawing her own strength from a deep faith in the Lord and bringing all the children up with a powerful sense of the reality of God.

By his early twenties, though, Damien was going through a very troubled time in his personal life, and began to question many things including his faith. He and his brother Gerald with sister Josie had set up in business together running the hotel in Newry, and in 1971 it was bombed for the first time. It was to be bombed five times in all and each time there was the infinitely depressing job of clearing up all the mess and trying to rebuild. After one particularly bad bomb attack, Damien spent months sitting alone in the little gate lodge at the bottom of the hotel drive, filling in endless forms and wondering what on earth life was all about. Soon it became clear that Gerald was feeling disillusioned and confused, too, and searching for some sort of meaning in his life. Damien wasn't sure if it was the answer, though, when Gerald started to show an interest in something called the "charismatic renewal" but he allowed himself to be persuaded to go up to Belfast to meet Frank Forte, one of the founder leaders of the Roman Catholic charismatic movement in Ireland. They went to a prayer meeting at which Damien felt very uncomfortable. It was the first time he had come into contact with people praising God aloud with words like "hallelujah", and, even stranger, he found them "praying in tongues". But he stuck it out and afterwards they went to a Christian coffee bar/restaurant run by Frank Forte. The three of them got chatting and Damien was thinking that Frank Forte didn't seem so cracked after all, when, suddenly, he suggested that they pray together right there in the middle of the restaurant! Damien was horrified. But he couldn't escape as in a second Frank had taken their hands in a firm grip and was praying out loud. Damien sat writhing in embarrassment, and couldn't believe it when afterwards Gerald said he was interested to find out more. They went back home, but somehow, despite Damien's resolve to steer clear of these rather "peculiar" people, the Lord had other plans and he found himself being hauled off to weekly meetings at the Quaker hall in Dublin on a Friday night, where people from all denominations met together to praise and worship God in whatever way they wanted. Damien had never experienced this sense of freedom before. At first he was sceptical, putting it all down to emotional hysteria led by extroverts – and it jarred on his reserved, conservative temperament. But as he saw people being physically and emotionally healed, set free from all sorts of bondages, and saw relationships and marriages being restored, he lost his cynicism, and eventually himself came into a deeper experience of the Holy Spirit.

It wasn't easy for him. There was a lot in his own life that needed to be healed and sorted out, and the months ahead were a hard test of whether it was all real. Since then, we've both seen how often an experience of this kind is followed by a period of trial and difficulty which we now recognise as spiritual attack. It was the same with Jesus when He was tempted by the devil in the wilderness immediately after being baptised by John in the Jordan. At the time, Damien went through a lot of private struggle, but at the end of it he knew he had found the one thing which gave meaning and fulfilment to life, and that was why he was prepared to risk our friendship to try to share it with me.

But I just couldn't understand what had come over him. I felt almost as if I'd been betrayed. How could this possibly have happened to Damien? Besides, any people I had heard speaking in charismatic terms had been non-Catholics, and it made me feel strangely insecure to think that the movement had "infiltrated" the comfortable confines of my own Church. In fact, I gradually became aware that thousands of Catholics in England and Ireland were being caught up into the new movement of the Holy Spirit which was sweeping through every denomination. In 1975 Pope Paul VI in Rome gave his blessing to the charismatic renewal within the Church, acknowledging the direct, personal relationship with God people were discovering. Yet I just couldn't open myself to that experience. Since I'd got all excited about things after talking with Jean Darnell and then been looked at like a person with two heads, I'd become cynical and uncomfortable about anything that looked like emotional hysteria. I felt I'd been let down once, and I certainly wasn't going to jump on a bandwagon now.

All the same, I was forced to look at my life long and hard. And the first thing I saw was that I needed to do a lot of growing up. I couldn't go on burying my head in the sand, pretending to be blind to the long-term effects of what I was doing. When you're a teenager, there is always tomorrow. Something new comes along, and the mistakes you make one day can be put right or forgotten the next. No one expects you to be all that reliable or sorted out, and adults will always bale you out if you get into deep water. But now it hit me like a bolt of lightning that I was entirely responsible for my own life, and that the relationships I formed now were in my hands to break or sustain for a lifetime. I had to wake up and start taking control of where my life was going, particularly where it affected other people. In a flash I decided to cut all ties with things that I felt couldn't last or were potentially hurtful to other people. Putting that into practice was far more difficult.

I knew I had to finish any relationship that I could see no future in and that included Damien. I was sure that what I was doing was the best and most honest thing for both of us but I was dreading Damien's reaction. I went down to his hotel and miserably poured out how I felt, that I respected and admired him but couldn't see myself as his wife. I was stunned at how understanding and generous he was. Instead of protests and recriminations, he said that he respected my decision and hoped we could remain friends. Then he suggested that since I was there it was a shame to waste the evening, so why didn't we have dinner together before saying goodbye?

I was only too happy to agree so out we went to a nearby restaurant for a meal and had a wonderfully relaxed time together, chatting and laughing like old friends about any old nonsense. I happened to mention that I'd never been to a typical Irish dance hall.

"You haven't lived if you haven't been to one of those,"

Damien replied, and very soon we were heading off to a remote little village in Donegal.

When we got there the dance was in full swing. We could hear John Glen and the Mainliners halfway down the street. There were cars parked everywhere, and heaps of bicycles piled up outside the hall. We queued in the rain to get our tickets, and once inside it was every man for himself. The place was jam-packed to the doors with all ages, shapes and sizes. I'd never seen anything like it. Before each set, the girls lined up along one wall and the boys stood opposite them about three feet away, eyeing them up and down and deciding which lucky girl they were going to dance with next. I couldn't believe my eyes. Damien suggested that just for a joke why didn't I go and line up with the other girls and he'd come and ask me to dance. Like a fool, I padded off and stood feeling very self-conscious, hoping that Damien would be quick, when suddenly my arm was seized by a thin spotty youth who demanded, "Are you dancing?" Before I could answer, I was hauled out on to the dance floor just as I caught sight of Damien sailing past with a stunning blonde, grinning all over his face. For a moment I was dumbstruck, then I saw the funny side of it and soon could hardly stand up for laughing. It seemed incredible that a man could play a joke like that on the same night he had had his marriage proposal rejected. I had expected the evening to be a total disaster, yet here I was laughing more than I'd done in months. Suddenly something broke inside me. As I watched him whirling round the room, I realised, like someone waking from a dream, that of all the men I knew, there was no one I'd rather be with than Damien. All the feelings that I'd been pushing down for the past three years came rushing to the surface and I knew that I loved him.

It was a new start for us. Over the coming months we spent more time together than we had over the past year. We had a lot to learn about each other and as we got to know each other more and more, our relationship grew deeper and warmer. There was just one shadow over our happiness though. Sometimes Damien would suggest we pray together, but I always felt embarrassed and uncomfortable. I realised that this could be a major obstacle for us – my feeling so cynical about something he felt so strongly – and I began to wonder how we would deal with this problem. Then something even bigger happened which took the matter out of my hands.

I suppose all of us tend to take our health for granted. As a singer, you'd become a nervous wreck if you worried all the time about how much depended on your voice. So, even though I'd had a certain amount of annoying throat trouble ever since my teens, I'd never thought too seriously about the possibility of losing my voice completely. In 1971, my voice had gone for the first time, and the problem was diagnosed as an irritation on the left vocal chord. The trouble seemed to clear up after a couple of weeks, but it recurred every year, each time slightly worse, until in 1975 my throat started haemorrhaging. I had an operation in which the surgeon cauterised the chord in the hope that this would heal the weakness. I wasn't able to speak for one and a half weeks, and it was a month before my voice came back, very weak and shaky.

That year was my busiest and most successful, and I was aware that I was putting not only my voice but my whole body under a lot of strain. I kept promising I'd take a break some time or cut down on my commitments, but somehow my diary kept getting filled with non-stop engagements. In September 1976, about a year after that first operation, I was rehearsing for a children's TV programme in Manchester. I had just released a single called "Fairytale" and was to sing it on the show but when I started to sing I found that I couldn't get any sound out on some low and high notes. I thought it was simply a bit of huskiness that would wear off, but by the afternoon I had almost no voice left and was reduced to a thick whisper. Something seemed to tell me this was more than just an ordinary sore throat. I had to act quickly.

Feeling strangely anxious, I travelled straight down to London to see the specialist who had been looking after me, a brilliant man called Alfred Alexander. I was shocked when he told me there was now a growth on the weak spot of my left vocal chord and he would have to operate immediately. My poor parents were devastated. Just a fortnight before my father had suffered a heart attack and was only just beginning to recover. It seemed incredible that there should be two members of the family in hospital with major surgery. We all hoped it was a false alarm and my parents asked for a second opinion that same day. It confirmed the worst. By the evening, I was in St Vincent's Clinic in Paddington and on the following morning the growth was being removed.

I'm glad it all happened so quickly. Cancer. The very word is enough to strike fear and dread into your heart. But by the time I was conscious enough really to entertain the possibility, I had been told the growth had not been malignant. In fact, the next day when I read newspaper headlines such as "SURGEON BATTLES FOR DANA'S VOICE", "DANA MAY NEVER SING AGAIN", and even "DANA FIGHTS FOR LIFE", I thought everyone was making a huge fuss, and I put it all down to media exaggeration.

Soon I realised that they weren't so far wrong. I suppose I had thought I would be back singing again in a few weeks just like after my little operation the year before, but Dr Alexander came in that morning and made it clear that this was a much more serious situation. In order to remove the root of the growth, he had been forced to take away a small part of the chord itself. Apparently this would affect the action of the chord and therefore the sound it produced – a drastic thing for a singer. However, he was pleased with the way the operation had gone, and all we could do now was wait until the chord healed. There was only one chance for my voice – TOTAL SILENCE.

I wasn't allowed to speak at all for three weeks and was warned that I could only use my voice sparingly over the following months. The prospects of continuing my career didn't seem that good. Yet I was determined to sing again. And two things in particular helped me in my struggle to get better. One was the support of all my family, friends and the public. I was just overwhelmed by people's kindness and concern. Soon my room was so full of flowers that I began to get hay fever and eventually most of them had to be removed. The media followed my progress with great interest, producing a flood of letters from well-wishers I would never meet, though I did try and reply to them. I carried on lengthy and often hilarious conversations on a pad of paper with my never-ending flow of visitors. One dear old lady got confused by this strange method of communication and thought she had to write her answers to me on the same piece of paper. My parents were so good, despite their own worries over Dad's illness, and made me even more determined to be positive and cheerful, and to follow the doctor's instructions for a speedy recovery.

The other thing which pulled me through was Damien. He came rushing over from Ireland as soon as he heard the news, grabbing the last drooping bunch of flowers from the shop down the street and creeping cautiously into my room, only to stand there embarrassed when confronted by something resembling the Chelsea Flower Show. It was difficult to reassure him that the state of his flowers didn't matter a jot. The important thing to me was that he was there. Soon he had relaxed and was filling me in on all the home news. Damien's hotel had been bombed again earlier in the year, another traumatic experience even though no one had been hurt, so he was in the middle of piecing his life together once more and trying to build up the business again. It had left me with even more respect for him as I knew there was nothing glib in anything he said about God. When he talked about God's love and power that day, I realised afresh that he had been through enough suffering for it to be something very real. His visit left me thinking a lot about where I stood with God.

Yet I found that I couldn't pray that my voice would come back again. Instead I prayed that I'd accept whatever God wanted for me. Now I know this sounds like the ideal spiritual thing to do – I thought so too at the time! – but I know, looking back, that I was actually afraid to ask for my voice back. What if, even after praying, I *wasn't* able to sing again? Would that confirm the niggling doubts that sprang into my mind at odd times, even when I was praying – is anyone really there? Does God really exist? Would I then be left knowing there was nothing? I was scared to face that possibility, and so I just prayed that I would be able to accept God's will – and *hoped* that everything would turn out all right.

At first it looked as though my luck would hold. It was lovely to be able to spend so much unexpected time at home and I hope I was able to give my parents some moral support during Dad's illness. Not being able to talk for three weeks was frustrating (almost a miracle in itself!) but it was fun to be able to potter around my own home doing things that I'd put off for months, even years, as life had grown more busy, things like oil painting and learning the harp. And eating! I put on nearly half a stone in weight over the next few weeks with Mum making sure I "kept my strength up". It was a luxury, too, being able to lounge about in jeans and sweatshirts instead of having to dress up each day. I had interviews to do, though, which I'm sure must have been amusing to watch – me answering questions on a piece of paper and the reporter either speaking in a hushed whisper, or bellowing at me as if I was stone deaf or daft in the head.

Soon I progressed to a whisper, and then I was allowed to speak normally with a little gentle singing for about ten minutes each day. It was a bit of a shock to find my voice sounding quite different and doing the most extraordinary things. When I sang certain notes two notes would come out. I was the only singer in the world who could harmonise with herself! But the doctor was optimistic about a full recovery and I assumed it was a question of time and patience. He predicted that by Christmas I would be almost back to normal, and so I didn't cancel the pantomime I was booked for – *Cinderella* in Manchester with Billy Dainty. I couldn't do any live shows that autumn and early winter but I was able to go to Japan in November to promote the Japanese version of "Cold, Cold Christmas" because in Japan I was allowed to mime to the record. But despite my limited appearances, my career seemed to be blossoming. The public, the press, the people in show business and the music world were all so kind. My record "Fairytale" was now No. 13 in the charts and I was inundated with requests for shows and appearances.

I became known as the Woman with the Bionic Voice because it was just incredible how the technicians managed to cover up my slips and weaknesses, and piece together scraps of recordings to give quite a respectable sound. But my nerves were getting affected by all the uncertainty. I was so embarrassed at having to keep cancelling work and, of course, each time it happened it received publicity. The thought of starting live work again scared me stiff.

My confidence was beginning to fade away. I couldn't see how I would manage my next project. I had to record a new single and Dick Leahy had found what he thought was just the right song, "Put Some Words Together" written by Tony McCauley, a man who had written an incredible number of hits, most recently David Soul's first No. 1, "Don't Give Up on Us, Baby".

The idea was to record the single in Los Angeles where Tony was recording an album with David Soul. Obviously I was very eager to do it, and everyone felt that if we took our time with the recording, my voice would be able to cope. As my mother had been under a great deal of strain over the past months, I thought it would be good for her to come with me now that my father was feeling much stronger. She could do with relaxing in the Californian sunshine – and I could do with her support.

It was a wonderful experience. We stayed in the beautiful Beverly Hills Hotel for three weeks and recorded the single in the studios originally owned by Charlie Chaplin. In our free time, we visited the sets of *Starsky and Hutch* and met David Soul and Paul Michael Glaser, which was a real thrill as I was a big fan. When they had finished filming that day, we all went to see the debut appearance of a new group. It turned out to be Blondie.

But it wasn't all fun and games. I found the recording extremely difficult and tiring. I was very tense and my throat would ache terribly after only a few minutes' singing. Still, with a lot of patience on the behalf of the producer we finished the single. But at what price? By the time we flew back to England, my voice was extremely weak so yet again we had to cancel all engagements. The specialist looked grave when he examined my throat, and I felt numb when he told me the vocal chords were dangerously inflamed and sore, and I would have to go back to total silence.

I began to wonder if I would ever be able to speak properly, let alone sing again. But the Lord was there once more. As I was slowly able to whisper again, David Winter of BBC Radio asked me to present a thirteen-week Christian radio programme called *I Believe in Music*. I had mixed feelings about it, quite apart from the uncertainty over my voice. Cliff Richard had presented it earlier, in a very direct evangelistic style with lots of gospel songs and Bible readings. I was dubious about too much Christian content and would have felt easier with more secular music. David was very understanding and allowed me to present the programme in whatever way I felt most comfortable. More important to me, I found I could talk quite openly to him about my fears and uncertainties concerning God. As the series drew on, I could hear a gradual improvement in the quality of my speaking voice.

The improvement was slow and unstable though. My vocal chords were so damaged that over the summer I began to feel more and more convinced I would never sing properly again. It became harder all the time to appear cheerful and optimistic, but mostly I managed to keep the mask up so that my friends and family wouldn't see how low I was getting. By the middle of August, I had reached rock bottom. I was supposed to appear in cabaret in a couple of months' time and it was being hailed as my comeback, yet here I was, unable to sing for longer than five minutes at a stretch. On one day of awful blackness, I felt I'd lost all hope. I sat down in the kitchen of the empty house and for the first time ever I experienced a feeling of total despair. I had fought for so long to get my voice back, and now it seemed as if I had lost the battle. Nobody seemed to be able to help my voice. I had to face the truth. I would never sing again. I felt exhausted and drained – too tired even to cry. I must have sat there for some hours. I wasn't aware of time. My mind seemed to be empty and I felt totally alone. All along I had resisted asking God to help me. Then, suddenly, without thinking, I found myself crying out, "God, if you're there, you've got to do something because I just can't do any more."

The heavens didn't open. There was no flash of lightning. But within seconds a thought came into my head – ask the specialist to recommend a singing teacher. It didn't seem a very dramatic miracle. In fact, it didn't seem like a miracle at all. My immediate thought was, why didn't I think of that before? The specialist wouldn't recommend anyone who wasn't good. So I dialled his number straight away. I couldn't believe it when he said that for the past two weeks he had been thinking of me and of a singing teacher, Florence Norberg. She was a world-famous teacher of many celebrated artistes, including Kiri Te Kanawa, and the specialist felt that her distinctive style of teaching could be the instrument to coax my voice back to life. I rang her immediately but didn't say who I was, only that I was "just a pop singer". I remember her crisp reply so vividly. "Never say 'just a pop singer'," she rapped. "A singer is a singer." The next day I presented myself for my first lesson.

It was a new beginning for me. Madame Norberg was exactly what I needed. Over the coming months, she not only enabled me to sing again but she gave me fresh hope and confidence. Madame Norberg was an exponent of the Viennese method of singing, and at first I was very suspicious as the techniques of my previous teachers had been anything but helpful. In fact, before the operation on my throat I hadn't had a single lesson, but it was important afterwards to learn how to breathe correctly and pitch the sound in such a way that it didn't harm the chord further. So I had at last approached a couple of teachers, with almost disastrous results. Madame Norberg, however, soon won my trust and respect. One thing which drew us close was that she had been through a very similar throat problem and had now not only recovered but had learnt a way of singing which enabled her to overcome any recurrent weakness or illness. At the beginning, when I was sometimes almost in tears at the awful croaking sound I was making, she would fill me with courage. "Don't listen to your voice," she would command, "listen to me." "I don't want your voice, I want your mind," she would drum into me every lesson. "If your mind does as I say, your voice will follow."

It really worked. I was so sceptical about anything new that I used to question everything she told me, and each time she would give me a clear, biological answer that I could really understand – not some airy-fairy reply about imagining emptying a tin of baked beans down your throat or anything weird like that. I was longing to learn and she was full of enthusiasm and encouragement, even before I noticed any improvement. It was hard, hard work since she was as determined as she was gentle and patient, and she wouldn't let me give up. I would come away from her house after each lesson feeling like I'd been knocked around a ring, but gradually I did notice the new strength and control in my voice. The sound was different, lower generally, yet at the same time I could reach higher notes than before, and some people said it had a greater richness and character.

I couldn't get away from the fact that God really had answered my prayer. He was there – and He cared for me, too. Gradually my fears and uncertainties began to diminish though I knew I still had a way to go before I could give myself to God completely. The next hurdle was to sing in public again. Kevin Shergold, a close friend in the Arts Centre Group, the organisation that brings together professional artists who are also committed Christians, had organised a small concert for me in his local church hall in the autumn, and that really helped to break the ice in getting me back into singing. It was a private cabaret party for invited friends, and I asked them to tell me honestly how I sounded. They were very encouraging and my confidence slowly began to return. In December I went live on the public stage for the first time at Caesar's Palace, Luton, and found myself playing to packed houses every night. There were several TV appearances around Christmas, and in January that radio series *I Believe in Music* went out. A tour of Ireland was followed by a Christian concert for ACG with Cliff Richard, Roy Castle and Neil Reid, a St Patrick's Day show on ITV and then an appearance in April on *The Rolf Harris Show*. My voice was holding its own. Life had turned a corner.

10

Throughout all this difficult time, Damien had been a tower of strength, coming with me to singing lessons whenever possible, telling me how well I was doing even when, to me, my voice sounded disastrous, phoning me every day when he couldn't be with me. Despite all his own problems with his hotel, he had been an endless source of encouragement and our love for each other had deepened even though I still didn't fully share his Christian commitment. When Damien was at home in Newry, he spent a lot of time at the Rostrevor Renewal Centre just down the road, an amazing Christian community run by Rev. Cecil Kerr, which drew together Catholics and Protestants to worship in unity and love. But I still remained unsure, even after my experience of God answering prayer the previous August. I hadn't got over feeling threatened and embarrassed by this freer, more personal way of talking about God – it seemed a bit emotional and intense to me – and I still had an idea that you had to be a really good sort of person to have that kind of relationship with God. I know I was too mixed up.

It seemed God knew all about that too. Later in 1977, I had been visiting Damien's family when he suggested that I talk to one of his brothers, the priest, Father Kevin, about the fears I had about the charismatic renewal. I had known Kevin for years. I liked him very much and we got along well together, yet for some strange reason I suddenly felt very nervous at the thought of talking to him. Still, I agreed rather reluctantly, and we got together that evening with me feeling very tense. He suggested that we start with a prayer, and before I could protest, he had closed his eyes and begun. Almost at once, an awful feeling of panic came over me. Somehow Kevin must have sensed it because he stopped in mid-sentence and after studying my miserable face for a few moments, he said gently, "I think the Lord wants us to talk."

I was so surprised. It seemed to me he must have been reading my mind and that gave me such a jolt that my defences fell and I found myself pouring out all my fears while Kevin just listened quietly. It was such a relief to share with someone, the fear and yet the longing. I knew my fear was irrational – what was there to be afraid of, after all? – but I just couldn't bring myself to let go completely and trust God with all of my life. Kevin reassured me a lot simply by saying that it was a perfectly normal, understandable reaction from someone who had been used to being independent and yet who, deep down, felt inadequate and unsure of her worth.

He was very wise and didn't pressurise me to come to some sort of decision about my commitment to God, but it looked as though God wasn't going to let me get away that easily. An extraordinary thing happened three weeks later. I was staying in Damien's hotel when a nun and priest arrived from Belfast where they had been praying with a girl who had lost both her legs after her car had been booby-trapped by mistake. Now, my instinctive desire is to like people, and normally I would say that even if a person appears really unpleasant, you can generally find something good about them, or at least understand their problems in terms of some past unhappiness. I hate any sort of bad atmosphere or tension between people, and I've always been the one to act as go-between to patch up quarrels.

But for some reason I took an instant dislike to this poor nun and priest. Everything about them irritated me to screaming pitch. Horrible thoughts kept coming into my head, and I found myself being critical about the most ridiculous things – like the priest's voice, his hands, even the way he ate; when

I looked at the sweet, innocent nun, all I could see was a little chattering rabbit. Dinner was agony. I felt so claustrophobic, and my nerves were going to shreds as I found the pair more and more irritating. To my horror, a prayer meeting was suggested after the meal, and it didn't seem possible to get out of it without really offending everyone. I felt like a trapped animal. As we went upstairs, every step was like going to my execution. A real sense of terror began to well up again. Once settled in the room, I nearly died when, after a time of singing and praise, all of them, Damien included, started to pray in tongues. I felt very frightened and my heart began to pound in my ears. All I could think was that it sounded like African tribal worship. I really had to shake myself then and try to drag myself out of my terrible narrow-mindedness.

With a great effort, I forced myself to calm down and be objective. I looked at the people sitting round me, mostly Damien's brothers and sisters. I knew them all and they were good people, normal, down-to-earth. Suddenly I realised they were gathering round to pray for me but I couldn't get out as I was wedged between the priest and the nun. I tried not to cringe as the priest held my hand, and the nun placed hers lightly on my shoulder. Quietly the priest began to pray. I couldn't believe my ears. This wasn't the same person. Here was a poet. What he actually prayed is lost to me now, but I just remember the most beautiful words streaming over me as if they were washing me right through, wonderful things about God's love for me. As the words poured over me, I felt an extraordinary bubbling sensation in my stomach which seemed to spread through my whole body, right up to my face, a feeling of joy and happiness like I'd never known. I wanted to smile, to laugh even. Soon I found myself joining everyone else in praising and thanking God. It was as if a great weight was being lifted away, and I became aware that now I felt at peace where before I had been closed and hurt. By the time we finished praying, I just couldn't grin wide enough, and I realised I had been squeezing the priest's hand so long and hard that I must have nearly broken it. I couldn't get over the tremendous sense of happiness I felt. The whole room seemed different. I felt completely at ease with Father Maher and Sister Josephine. I even felt a deep sense of love for them.

It was me who had changed – and my whole life from that moment on. In the days ahead, I found a new excitement and meaning in my spiritual life. I began to see God much more as my Father and friend, a real person, someone I could turn to and share my fears and insecurities with. And I've never lost that relationship. In fact, it has grown deeper and stronger over the years. I know that God loves me and cares for me. He gives me what I need. More than that, He gives me what is *best* for me and at the *time* that is best for me. In the early days, I would be so surprised at the extraordinary coincidences that would happen. The list is endless, but to give just one tiny example, a friend came to our home to lunch one day. He had been suffering from depression for many years and although he had received lots of treatment including electric shock and hospitalisation, he just couldn't get free of it. As we talked it became clear to us that the root cause lay in his past. He had bitter, painful memories of things which had happened to him when he was younger. Damien and I agreed that if only we could arrange for him to meet Kevin, we just knew that he would be helped as Kevin had a special gift in the healing of memories. But Kevin was living and working down in Dublin at that time and we hadn't seen him for several months. Then, about half an hour later, the phone rang and it was Kevin. He was just passing through Newry and wanted to call in and see us! I just couldn't believe it. He came straight round and spent a few hours talking with our friend who, thankfully, is now healed of his depression and tells us that his meeting with Kevin was the beginning of the road back for him.

In my own life, the Lord has helped me to deal with all aspects of my character. For example, I've always found decision-making a problem. Usually I'm able to see both sides of an argument. And when it comes to taking some action, I always want to know as far as possible how my decision will affect me – where will it take me? Will I be able to stand by what I've decided? By the time I've thought all these things out, the problem has often decided itself. God has shown me that the first thing I must do is *trust* Him and talk to Him about the choice I have to make – in other words, I need to pray about it. There's great strength in praying with other people, too, so that's what I do. I tell the Lord about the problem, asking Him to direct me, and confirm what I should do through discerning people who share my beliefs and values.

I must say, though, that God's decision isn't always in agreement with my own feelings on the matter! I've often felt very negative about things which, in retrospect, have been so right and intended for me. In these cases, I've had to learn to "step out in faith" – which means exactly that. I've had to go ahead, in the dark sometimes, just trusting that God knows what is best for me, even if it hasn't made sense to me or I've actually felt against the idea. I'm seeing more and more that if God is leading me in a certain direction, it's best to go. On the occasions I've done this, it has been remarkable how the seemingly impossible is achieved so easily – and you'll see examples of this as my story goes on. It's like seeing the pieces of a jigsaw coming together just at the right time, and I've learnt now that there are no "coincidences" with God. He has everything planned for me.

Obviously what I experienced that day in Damien's hotel put a whole new dimension into my relationship with him. But it didn't mean it was plain sailing from there. We still had a great deal to work out together. Our lifestyles and careers were so different. Or, at least, so we thought at first, but we learnt that there were incredible similarities between show business and hotel business. They both dealt with entertaining the general public; just as with artistes, hotel managers couldn't have "off days" – the show had to go on; and, of course, we both worked unsociable hours. I still had the idea, though, that Damien was quite self-sufficient, and my own low self-esteem sometimes made it hard for me to believe I had anything to offer. (I mean, you can't sing all the time, can you?!) Anyway, Damien seemed sure about us and over the winter and the spring of 1978 we became more and more deeply committed to each other. At Easter we privately decided to marry.

The press had picked up rumours of the romance over a year before, and when we attended my brother Gerald's wedding at St Eugene's Cathedral in Derry together, it was difficult to keep our attachment secret. The next day the papers were full of the probability that we would be the next couple down the aisle. I'm afraid we left them guessing. Neither of us wanted too much fuss and publicity but in the end we decided the best thing to do would be to make an announcement to the press in July, by which time the arrangements for our October wedding would be well in hand.

Damien was very nervous about his first official press meeting, but he needn't have worried. In all the interviews he came across as so genuine and open that the reporters warmed to him straight away. However, there was one thing he found particularly embarrassing – the fact that I had refused to have an engagement ring, a point not missed by the hawk-eyed press. The truth was that once we had made our personal commitment to marry, I didn't see the need to wear an engagement ring – it just seemed a waste of money to me. But at the press interview, we all had a good laugh at Damien's expense when he admitted he was afraid people would think he was too mean to buy one! It was a very happy and relaxed few hours, and I quite enjoyed being upstaged by my tall, handsome fiancé.

Life was certainly hectic, but my voice seemed to be coping with the strain. I suppose it was difficult organising my professional comeback on the one hand, and trying to arrange my own wedding, now so close, on the other. But one thing I've learnt in life is to live one day at a time. Along with everything else, I was in the middle of recording a new album, "The Girl is Back". It was an exhausting but exciting project. Madame Norberg had done wonders with my voice but I was still apprehensive about causing more damage to the delicate vocal chords, so the recording was slow and laborious. The exciting part, though, was that the album presented a whole new musical image and style. I was lucky enough to have Barry Blue as my producer for the album, and even more privileged that he devoted a year to me almost exclusively between working out new material and recording.

Barry, famous as a writer/pop singer himself, had turned record-producer after spending many years in music publishing. Dick Leahy invited him to produce the debut album of a new group he had found called Heatwave. It turned out to be a platinum album in America. It was after this that he produced my new record. I think he saw it as a challenge, seeing potential for development into more adventurous musical styles, much more sophisticated and up-tempo, even rocky. Barry wrote several of the tracks, and John and Gerald also contributed some songs. It was hard work but we had many magical moments and lots of laughs during the months we worked together. We finally finished recording one very tired morning at 7 a.m., exactly two weeks before my wedding.

During this mad month, most of the moments Damien and I did manage to grab together were spent planning the wedding and getting our new home ready. We had bought a beautiful old Georgian house at the foot of the lovely Mountains of Mourne on the banks of Carlingford Lough. Set in eight acres of mature lawns and shrubs, with quaint walled gardens, the four-bedroomed, one-storey house was tranquil and secluded. We had decided I would have a break from professional engagements for a while, and I was looking forward with a mixture of apprehension and excitement to transforming the dusty, neglected house and dilapidated stables and barns into a model of beauty and productivity. There was no question of resentment or regret at the prospect of becoming a housewife. My life with Damien was far more important to me than my career, and I felt instinctively that it was vital for our relationship and my own self-respect that I gave all my attention to the task of creating a home and giving Damien all my support. I suppose some women might be up in arms reading this, but it was basic to my sense of fulfilment as a woman that I managed all the housework myself.

At times, though, I was filled with panic. I respected and loved Damien deeply, but every now and then I would be overwhelmed by the seriousness and responsibility of what we were undertaking. For both of us, marriage was a lifetime commitment. Divorce just wasn't a possibility to me, no matter how tough things might get, so I wasn't under any illusions that if it didn't work out we could just scrap it and start again. I somehow felt that there ought to be a bolt of lightning or a voice from heaven as confirmation that we should go ahead with getting married. During these moments of terrified doubt, I would ask every married woman I knew, "How did you *know* your husband was the right man?" but there didn't seem to be any magic formula. It seemed to be another area where you just had to have faith that you were doing what the Lord wanted for you. And I realise now that a successful marriage isn't like a one-armed bandit machine where, if you're simply lucky enough to get the right combination, the jackpot comes tumbling out. Marriage is something which is built, not ready-made, brought into being often through a lot of hard work and sacrifice. And I can see, too, that there isn't a finished product. You've never "made it" – which is both the challenge and the joy of marriage.

11

The day fixed for the wedding was October 5th, 1978.

In the week before, Damien and I arranged to give a number of parties, among them one for all my family and relations, and one for his. That sounds quite harmless, but as one of fifteen children, Damien had a list which seemed to run into hundreds, and we just couldn't fit them all in my parents' house. The other complication was that we wanted to do the catering ourselves, and cooking wasn't my strong point. That is an understatement. I was clueless. Because I'd always had so much music and dancing practice to do as a child, Mum had let me off most of the household chores, and since then I'd always been living with them or staying in hotels. Now I was determined to improve my culinary skills, and, being born into a strong tradition of generous hospitality, I set to work making enough salads, cakes and puddings to feed an army. I soon discovered there was more to this cooking business than met the eye. You would have thought it was impossible to burn boiled eggs – but I managed it. Good and hard was how you wanted them for a salad – so on the afternoon of the party I let them boil for five hours. As the water bubbled away, I just kept topping the saucepan up again. When I finally rescued them, the water had disappeared and the whites of the eggs had turned dark brown! I felt such an idiot. Luckily, my sisters were there, waving magic wands of efficiency, helped by my uncle Mixie, and soon there was a marvellous spread on the tables. I was relegated to making the tea, but when I carried out the first pot triumphantly and went to pour, I discovered I had forgotten to put the water in. Fortunately only Damien was around to see, and he just roared with laughter when I turned scarlet with embarrassment.

The week sped by with rehearsals and meetings for work and wedding on both sides of the Irish Sea. The night before, at a rehearsal of the actual ceremony at St Eugene's Cathedral, we were asked if we had arranged crush-barriers. The idea shocked us as we had never imagined there would be any need for them, but we made some hasty arrangements for the church ushers to be there. Damien left, exhausted, at 11.30 p.m. In a kind of daze, I woke up at seven o'clock on the morning of the Great Day to a delicious breakfast of scones, baps, and lots of hot, weak tea brought in by my mother. The ceremony was at twelve noon, and all the preparations that had to be made by then left little time for panic. In fact, I think the rest of the family were more nervous than I was. Dad looked tense and uncomfortable in his formal clothes, and even Mum's normally unruffable calm was getting a bit frayed at the edges. Still, with Eileen's professional touch for my hair and make-up, all seemed to be going well – until about a quarter to twelve. My mother had left, and the car was waiting to drive Dad and me to the cathedral. I'd left putting on my dress until the last minute as I didn't want to crease it, and as I now eased myself into it gingerly, horribly conscious of all the extra pounds that had somehow crept on in the last few weeks, there was an awful tearing sound, and Eileen, who had been doing me up, leapt back with a small scream. The zip had broken. Poor Eileen started to shake so much that she couldn't begin to mend it, so Susan was called in. At first she thought it would simply be a question of undoing the bottom of the zip and retreading it, but too many teeth were broken higher up. There was nothing for it but to sew me painstakingly into the dress, leaving me terrified to breathe, and having to spend all day just taking little shallow gasps.

Thanks to Susan's skill and iron nerve, we set off only a few minutes late. We soon realised the delay wouldn't make much difference. As we approached the area near St Eugene's, I couldn't believe my eyes. Thousands of people packed the streets, whilst the grounds of the cathedral were a solid mass of excited, cheering well-wishers. It was overwhelming to see their open affection, but I began to get really worried as the car tried to edge its way into the crowd. People were so tightly piled together that it was impossible to force a path, and I was terrified that someone would be injured in the crush or fall under the car. Glancing up at Dad's grey face, I became even more scared about the strain it would be for him getting into the church. Far in front of us, I saw the ushers fighting to clear a way to the door, but eventually the car had to give up about thirty yards away, and Dad and I prepared to try and walk from there. As I scrambled out of the car, my head was jerked back as my veil got caught and then freed itself. By the time we reached the door, I was white as a sheet, hardly the traditional blushing bride.

Inside, the scene was incredible. There were so many people there, filling the aisles and even balancing *on top* of the confessional boxes. We had only invited four hundred guests. The air was buzzing with excitement, and the atmosphere was more like that of a carnival than a church service. It was overwhelming, but somehow Dad and I managed to stagger down to the altar in the centre of the nave around which were yet more people with the choir squeezed in on the right. I've never been so glad to see Damien's reassuring smile.

It was a most beautiful and moving service. I felt such a presence of the Lord there, and I wasn't the only one. Even our non-Christian friends said they sensed a very special atmosphere. A truly ecumenical Mass, it was graced by no fewer than three bishops, Dr Daly, ex-bishop Dr Farren, and the Church of Ireland bishop, whilst Cecil Kerr from the Rostrevor Renewal Centre read one of the lessons and Father Kevin married us as the fabulous choir sang like angels. There was just one strange thing. Damien and I were kneeling facing the congregation with the bridesmaids and groomsmen on either side. During the service, it seemed as if male members of the congregation kept disappearing. Each time I looked round the cathedral, more had vanished. I really thought I must be imagining it, but by the end of the service, only women seemed to be left. It didn't seem possible that every single man had had to answer the call of nature. But I soon discovered the solution to the mystery.

I had been so wrapped up in the beauty and awesomeness of the occasion that I'd forgotten the crowds outside. But as we walked blissfully down the aisle and out to the cathedral steps, it was like experiencing a volcanic explosion. A huge cheer erupted from the crowds packed into the grounds, and confetti began to shower down upon us like coloured rain. But holding back the surging flow of people were all the men who had slipped out during the service and were now forming a human chain. That saved us from being crushed to death after five minutes of married life, but they couldn't do anything about the crowds which lined the streets on the way to the reception. The factories and schools in Derry had been given a half-day holiday, and the route to the Everglades Hotel looked again like a carnival gathering. I shall never forget the love and support my own townsfolk gave me. It took nearly four hours to reach the reception, and then there were all the press interviews with three TV crews and dozens of foreign reporters, followed by all the official photographs. The poor hotel staff must have been tearing their hair out as the meal for four hundred guests had been booked for about two o'clock, but by some feat of magic, they produced a superb hot meal as if it were no more trouble than beans on toast when we finally sat down, ravenous, at six o'clock.

Damien and I had chosen all our favourite foods for the meal, and I wolfed down mine, especially the profiteroles, as if I had been starved. But poor Damien was almost sick with worry about his speech and could hardly eat a thing. He got through the ordeal, keeping it short and sweet, without anyone realising just how much his legs were shaking, while I took a welcome back seat and just sat praying silently for him. I wasn't allowed to escape that easily though, as when Damien sat down, sighing with relief, the dreaded cry went up, "Give us The Song!" And Damien pleaded, quick as a flash, "Just sing *one* verse," which brought a hoot of laughter.

The beautiful evening rushed by with frustratingly little time to talk properly to all the wonderful people there. At 10.30 p.m., we finally dragged ourselves away from a party which looked set to go strong for the rest of the night at least, and set off for Dublin. We never realised the car journey would take so long, and it was three in the morning before we arrived, shattered, at the Berkeley Court Hotel. By this time we were about ready to eat a horse, but to our horror we discovered the hotel had only just been opened and, as yet, room service was only available until 2 a.m. Mournfully, we munched our way through a bowl of fruit, the only food we could find, and toasted the departing wedding day with glasses of water.

The next day we flew to London, and then on to the Caribbean, stopping off in Barbados for another night before we finally landed at our destination, the lovely island of Grenada. We learnt later that back in Derry everyone was having a whale of a time, with the reception lasting three whole days! Mum and Dad had most people back to their house for a big buffet, and there, it seems, lifelong friendships were struck up over the cucumber sandwiches. As for us, we stepped out of our tiny island-hopper plane, stretching our aching knees which had been supporting all our luggage, and found ourselves in a paradise on earth.

Grenada was more beautiful than we had ever imagined, more idyllic than even the pictures in the holiday brochure suggested. As the taxi driver drove us along the winding mountain track near St George, we looked down in wonder at the lush vegetation and huge exotic flowers. Occasionally you caught a glimpse of a brightly coloured bird, or heard the lazy tinkle of goat bells on the hillside, but the overall impression was that time had stood still. I remember thinking on that journey to our hotel that the driver must have had a tortoise for a father, he drove so slowly, but three weeks later, on our way home, we both felt he must be speeding, our pace of life had relaxed so much since coming.

The Spice Island Inn lived up to its romantic name. You walked through the front entrance to find that it was just a portico leading straight on to a dazzling white beach, sun-scorched palm trees and a turquoise sea. The accommodation was in secluded little chalets with walled gardens leading on to a swimming pool. From the overhanging bedroom balcony, it would have been possible to dive straight into the shimmering water. There was only one drawback. Although we had expected Grenada to be hot, our chalet was stifling, and we used to joke that maybe the air conditioning was blowing out hot air. You shouldn't joke about things like that. Four days after we had arrived, the manager approached us almost on his knees, and begged forgiveness for the fault in the air conditioning which had been doing just that.

I suppose one blight on the holiday, though it had its benefits, was that I managed to get a nasty tummy bug. Damien and I were out shopping in a supermarket when I began to feel very sick and faint. I thought it was just the heat and didn't bother to call Damien who was in another part of the shop, but suddenly everything seemed to swim before my eyes, and I quietly passed out under the washing powder. I came round within seconds and found pandemonium reigning with half a dozen people calling for a doctor, several more for an ambulance, and Damien gazing down at me in anxious disbelief. I was carried into the manager's office where I was able to lie down until the arrival of a very smart and efficient young black doctor who turned out to have trained in Ireland and knew Dublin even better than we did. He had me carted off to the hotel where he diagnosed three different viruses and ordered me to take a week in bed with no solid food. That didn't sound much fun, but in fact it gave me a marvellous rest (my first in two years), and I felt a lot better in a few days. I also managed to lose a bit of the extra weight I'd gained before the wedding, and as Damien didn't succumb to the bug we stayed in fairly good spirits right through.

I was glad to be back in the swing of things, though, as the food was amazing, particularly the soups of every colour, flavour and consistency which were the speciality of the chef. There was one with mushrooms which I liked so much that I asked the cook for the recipe – and he sent me back one involving 40 lb. of potatoes, 29 lb. of onions, 14 lb. of mushrooms, etc., which tied me in knots trying to scale it down to the right proportions for two.

It seemed that Grenada was a home from home for the Irish. We found a little Catholic church on the first Sunday, and discovered there a congregation of nuns and priests from Dublin. It was like a big family reunion meeting them, and they overwhelmed us with kindness, taking us up into the mountains where their parish extended, and all round the island to little hidden communities that we would never have discovered otherwise. Everywhere we went, the people came out to stare and smile, and in one tiny settlement, all the children gathered round to sing to us.

We got to know a few of the people in the hotel, and on one occasion we hired a yacht to go out to the coral reef with three other couples. On the way out we stopped at a little uninhabited island for a picnic lunch and to practise snorkelling. I could hardly swim, let alone snorkel, so I spent most of the lunch break splashing around in the shallows like a beached whale. I thought I was doing really well and getting very daring, but with a mask on the seabed seems much further away, and when I put my foot down I discovered the water was only about nine inches deep! Still, I didn't need great expertise as later on we spent most of the time hanging on to the side of the boat and gazing down in wonder through our masks at fish like jewels which darted through the glowing forest of coral.

It was bliss to be able to relax and forget all about work and responsibilities for a while. But perhaps the most important benefit of the honeymoon was the way it drew Damien and me together. We'd always been aware of the differences in our characters and interests, so we had prayed especially that God would give us something to share. He gave us a song. Damien had no confidence at all in his musical ability as he had been told as a child that he was tone deaf. In fact, he has a sensitive musical ear, and simply needed a bit of encouragement. "Praise the Lord" was the first Christian song I had ever attempted, but there was nothing artificial or self-conscious about it. Somehow it just seemed to write itself out of the peace and joy that was between us and inside us. Basically, I got the melody and together we wrote the lyrics, but the final product was a blend of us both. At the time, I didn't think much more of it than that it was a lovely gift from the Lord that only the two of us would share. I had no idea it was the opening of a new dimension in my personal life and in my career.

Holidays always seem too short. We both felt we were just beginning to unwind when we found ourselves bumping once more down the pot-holed mountain road to start our reluctant journey home. And being at home came as quite a shock. As I've said, I was determined to do all my own housework and cooking, but the reality wasn't quite so straightforward. After the fiasco with the boiled eggs, I didn't have a huge amount of confidence in my culinary ability, and I was a little concerned that we couldn't very well live for ever on my five basics: vegetable soup, boiled bacon, meat and carrot stew, scrambled eggs and sherry trifle. I tried branching out – and found we either had enough macaroni cheese to cement a wall, or sat down to a dejected-looking lettuce leaf and a shrivelled scrap of meat. Damien often helped me, and being a hotelier, he could knock up a beautiful meal in a matter of minutes, but that sometimes left me feeling inadequate and stupid. Like the chip incident. I'd been hacking away laboriously at chunks of potato, almost carving out each chip individually, when Damien came into the kitchen and in a few devastating cuts and twists reduced the whole pile to immaculately even sticks. I felt useless. But I was determined to prove myself, and each night we fought our way through mountains of mashed potato, oozing with butter, and huge wedges of apple pie smothered in cream.

Entertaining was too daunting a prospect, so I refused to have a dining table, but I tried to make up for this cowardice by putting generous bowls of chocolates and nuts about the room. Unfortunately we found that, guests or no guests, the bowls had to be filled about six times a day, and it wasn't long before I discovered I had put on a stone in weight.

The washing was another phenomenon that took some mastering. We used to pile it all into our new automatic washing machine. That was fine, so effortless, and I did heaps of it in the first few weeks, opening the door of the spare bedroom when I got home and just flinging it in to wait for a free day to tackle ironing it all. When my sister-in-law came to stay, she offered to help out with some ironing for me and I gaily waved her in the direction of the spare room. She could barely get in. After much pushing and a scramble over the mountain of clothes, she set about it with her powerful right arm, but after four and a half hours she was still only about halfway through. That taught me about the unequal nature of washing and ironing, and since then we try to get through a load each day.

But these domestic hiccups weren't the only problems we had to overcome in the first year of marriage. I hadn't realised what a lot of growing up I had to do emotionally. Marriage really revealed to me what I was like deep inside, all the fears and inadequacies I'd been hiding from or hadn't been able to face. I knew Damien loved me but deep down I felt unsure of myself and very vulnerable. I found myself wondering if he was really happy with me or was he already regretting his choice of a wife? Damien was so good to me, very patient and gentle, but no matter how understanding he was, it didn't seem to give me the reassurance I needed. It never crossed my mind that *he* might be having similar problems in adjusting to married life.

Maybe it wouldn't have made any difference, though. When you feel a failure, you tend to feel guilty, too, guilty that you've let someone down, hurt the person you care most about. And I suppose there's nothing more crushing than feeling you're a disappointment to the person whose love and respect you want most. The trouble is it soon becomes unbearable, so that, without realising it, gradually you start trying to pass the blame on to your partner. You become critical and resentful. I would spend all day longing to hear Damien's step in the hall but when he did arrive, I would be cold and unresponsive though in my heart I longed to be warm and loving. There seemed to be a great barrier between us. Perhaps because I was afraid, I just couldn't give myself to him completely. I couldn't understand what was happening to me.

The saddest part was that at first I couldn't talk about it, not to Damien nor to anyone else. I've always found it very hard to talk about deeply personal things (and it's not easy being so honest now!) but I know that communication is absolutely vital if a marriage is to work. And by communication I mean making sure that your partner is hearing what you're *really* saying and vice versa. To begin with, it's essential to understand that your partner is not a mind reader. There's no point in guessing games. You need to explain exactly what you're feeling. But at the time, I became so withdrawn and lonely that I knew I couldn't talk to Damien or anyone about my feelings without bursting into tears. When he came home I couldn't even smile, and if he was twenty minutes late and the meal had been waiting, I would be furious one minute and crying the next. Damien tried to reassure me and tell me he loved me, but I was so depressed and confused I couldn't believe him. I felt no one could love such a selfish, unloving person as me.

But God could. I found it very difficult to pray during those dark early months but I did try to start each day by thanking God for the good things I had, starting with the things I took for granted, like the fact that I could walk and think and see. I would talk to Him about the irrational way I was feeling and ask Him to deal with it. When I did this, I always had a sense of God's love for me just as I was. But it was so hard to hold on to that fleeting sense of peace when things were difficult between Damien and me so God had to provide another way out for me. I got to know of a priest who was involved in marriage guidance, and he gave me some simple but effective advice. He told me to try and stop looking in on myself, at the effect of everything on *me*, and to look beyond to other people and their needs. He suggested that maybe Damien wasn't as confident as he appeared, and really needed my encouragement to be able to demonstrate his love for me more effectively. Because I felt so unlovable myself, I had painted an unreal picture of Damien as someone so strong and secure that he didn't need my reassurance and love. (It was the old story of "If you can't love yourself, you can't love anyone else".) This priest suggested imagining for a while that Damien wasn't my husband but one of my best friends so that when he came home in the evening I greeted him with affection instead of biting his head off. I remember feeling disappointed at his advice. I had expected an instant remedy, a wave of the magic wand. But I gave it a try, and although it took a great deal of effort and prayer, and the improvement was slow, I gradually learnt to control my negative feelings, and discipline myself to react warmly so that the love deep down had a chance to express itself and I could accept the love that was being given. I've often thought since then how strange it is that we can treat our friends better than we do our own partners and family, that we take more liberties with people who are very close to us and expect them to tolerate much more than people we love and depend on far less.

12

Luckily for most of this difficult period I was at home as I had cut my work down to an absolute minimum. After completing the album "The Girl is Back" in 1978, I did very little singing until early in 1979 when I began to stretch my wings a bit more – not because I felt restless but because, as usual, things just happened that way. In January I found I was voted Top Female Vocalist in the National Club Acts Awards for 1978–1979. In March I brought out a new single called "Something's Cooking in the Kitchen" for which I did a promotional video which was shown on *Top of the Pops* and other TV shows. The following month the album I'd worked so hard on, "The Girl is Back", was finally launched. By this time I had had my hair permed, changed my make-up to much more vibrant colours, and had a whole new wardrobe of clothes designed for me. Suddenly I found myself being interviewed by fashion magazines and women's journals about my "new image", though really it wasn't so much a conscious decision to create another identity as simply that I felt like changing my look. I was at a new stage in my life.

Records don't just spring into the charts overnight like mushrooms. They require a massive amount of publicity work so as well as television, radio and press promotion in Britain, we did a very hectic promotional tour of Europe on which Damien was able to accompany me. While we were courting, I was often so pressurised with work that I just couldn't remember what I'd done only the week before – or what I was doing the following one. Damien just couldn't understand this and used to get annoyed that I was so vague and didn't let him share in what I was doing. But when he came on this trip, he realised just how exhausting and confusing it all was. Afterwards he joked with his friends, quite truthfully, that one day he had breakfast in Hamburg, coffee in Cologne, lunch in Milan and dinner in Rome!

Later in the year I did a British concert tour which finished with my debut at the Royal Festival Hall. That was a wonderful experience. In June something quite different came up. I sang at the Roman Catholic Charismatic Conference in Dublin, my first time of standing up and making a public acknowledgment of my new experience of God. I felt very nervous, but it was impossible to be intimidated by the lovely people I met there. I felt shy and conspicuous going along to prayer meetings and discussion groups with people I didn't know as everyone else seemed to be able to praise and worship God so freely, whereas I still felt slightly embarrassed at first by all the singing and dancing "in the Spirit" as they called it. But I soon realised how genuine and natural it all was, and I quickly lost my inhibitions in the atmosphere of love and acceptance there. It was an amazing experience to join with thousands of Christians in the open air and express our thanks to God so spontaneously.

Then suddenly, that same month, disaster struck. Damien's hotel was blown up for the sixth time, and this time it was completely devastated. Mercifully no one was injured as the guests, staff and Damien's brother, Gerald, who lived in the flat on the top floor, had cleared the building in time. We knew it was in answer to prayer that through all the troubles and bombs of the past eleven years, no one had been hurt. We stood looking at the smoking shell, knowing it was the final blow. Apart from the new extensions at the rear of the building, the hotel was utterly destroyed. Everyone was shattered. There were many tears as the majority of the staff had worked there for fifteen years and some had worked for the family for even longer. Although no one said it, we were saying goodbye to the Ardmore Hotel. And to an era. It was especially hard for

Damien. Over the coming months, he felt a hopeless sense of responsibility to his staff. The place had been his "home" for so many years before our marriage. He'd really grown up there, learnt his trade and made so many friendships. Now he had to think of the future. Our future. We came through those months with a new understanding of each other and a stronger, deeper love.

Damien had known a priest called Father Raphael Short for three years. He ran a rehabilitation centre for alcoholics and drug addicts in Dublin, and Damien had had a strong interest in it for some time. When you are meeting people constantly in your hotel and spending time with them while they relax, they tend to open up to you and tell you their troubles. Every hotel manager gets to be a bit of a counsellor and psychologist. He can't help learning to read people, to see the sad man behind the joker, the insecure one behind the extrovert. People get to trust him, and there was a special charisma about Damien which drew people to confide in him. He was a good listener, but there was also a strength and stability, a peace about him which came partly from his natural gentleness, and partly from his faith in God.

Father Raphael felt that Damien had the right qualities to work with people suffering from deep problems and addictions, so he offered Damien a place on the counsellors' training course. It seemed so right. In October 1979 we moved into a three-bedroomed, semi-detached house in Dublin and began a very different way of life, living for the most part on Damien's salary of about £70 a week, and slowly learning a deeper compassion for people as we came into contact with the desperate cases which passed through the Centre. The policy of the Centre was that staff members themselves and, if possible, their partners too, should receive counselling so that the therapy they learnt to give flowed from a stability in their personal relationships and a fundamental self-awareness. The sessions I went along to with Damien taught me so much about myself, and helped to bring a freer communication between us which strengthened our relationship. As for

Damien, he found it tiring, even harrowing work at times, but extremely fulfilling and rewarding. Under Father Raphael's guidance, the Centre dealt with the healing of the whole person – physical, mental and particularly the spiritual healing that all alcoholics and drug addicts are searching for. Alcoholics Anonymous describes addiction as a physical, mental and *spiritual* disease, but so often, in treatment, the spiritual dimension is underplayed and sometimes ignored completely. Damien would tell me that there was a real presence of the Lord at particular group sessions where very deep healing had taken place. Even people there who didn't believe in God sensed that something wonderful was happening.

We stayed in Dublin for a year until Damien had completed his course and taken his final exams. I look back on that time as being a very special period in our lives. What we learnt and experienced during those months has been an invaluable help to us in our daily lives, in our marriage and in our relationship with our children. It also gave us a clearer idea of what the Lord wanted for our lives, and prepared us for the work He was leading us into.

There had been a change in my management by this time. It had been a terrible blow when my great friend Dick Katz had died, and with my father less active after his coronary, it was necessary to find another full-time manager. The answer was Jo Lustig, a talented American from Brooklyn who had impressed everyone by the dramatic way he took Mary O'Hara to stardom. He was a wizard in the folk field and a wonderful manager, particular, careful and protective. The only trouble was that I was now in middle-of-the-road pop, and I think also maybe I restricted Jo as I didn't want to do too much live work which would take me away from home. We parted two years later when Tony Cartwright, my present manager, took over.

During our stay in Dublin, I did very little career work, but I had to complete the recording of a Sunday morning religious BBC TV series for children called *Wake Up Sunday*. I loved every minute of it. I ended up making four series! We started recording the first one in February 1979, and it consisted of nine programmes which took me all round the country visiting primary schools and working with some lovely children. Each week the programme took a different theme – such as anger, fear, forgiveness or love – which was then illustrated in song, dance and drama. There were lots of beautiful contributions from the kids in spot interviews, a story from the Bible, and zany humour from Whizzy, a cartoon character from outer space. Yet there was a dignity and simplicity about it too. I remember one programme on the theme of "happiness". When I asked one little boy what made him most happy, he replied without hesitation, "What makes me happiest is to see my best friend smile." He was a blond Cockney lad; his friend was a black West Indian.

Damien and I had not written anything since "Praise the Lord" a year earlier, but just before Christmas we wrote our second song together. "Totus Tuus" was inspired by the motto of Pope John Paul II: "totus tuus" – totally yours, meaning completely dedicated to God. Sadly, I was recording *Wake Up Sunday* during the Pope's visit to Ireland in October, but I watched each huge gathering on the TV, and I was really struck by the love and dedication which passed between him and the Irish people, and yet his insistence that it was not to him but to the Lord that the love should be directed. When I came home, Damien said that he thought it would be lovely to write a song based on the Pope's motto, "Totally Yours". He felt that Christians should be able to say this to the Lord every day of their lives. Well, we tried to write a song but although we did pray about it, it turned out very wooden and sentimental, so we decided to forget the idea. Then one night we were driving to Newry and we passed the site of the Pope's visit to Drogheda. It made us think again about his visit and how he had brought with him such a feeling of love and peace. He had carried the Lord to the forefront and made young and old alike stop and think of their commitment to Him. Suddenly within about twenty minutes the new song "Totus Tuus" had almost written itself. It was a marvellous experience for us, after all the time and effort put into our first version, to have a new song now that was a deep and true expression of the faith that was at the centre of our lives, and we thought it would remain on that personal level. But lots of our friends thought it had a powerful message and enough musical merit to warrant being released as a single. Eventually we recorded it in the Windmill Studios in Dublin, using young semi-professional musicians as well as professional, and bringing in vocal backing by six boys and girls who normally sang in a church choir.

It seemed as if right from the start this was a song God had a special plan for – He must have wanted to bring some good out of it because the devil obviously wasn't too pleased about it. I had been making records for thirteen years by this time and had never encountered such unbelievable problems before. At first I thought we were just having a spot of bad luck. For example, we had to change studios halfway through recording, and, because of a mix-up, lost one full day of studio time. The next day, we had to abandon the second studio as the engineer couldn't get the equipment to work. (Later, because of our complaints, the studio was examined and no faulty machinery was discovered!) So we ended up going back to the first studio at 1 a.m. and working till 10 a.m. the next morning. And on top of this, all through the session our producer was very ill with apparent food poisoning.

We thought we'd had our fair share of "bad luck" but immediately we encountered more. My record company in England at the time didn't feel they could release a Christian record but gave permission for us to take it to another company of their choosing. This we did, collecting the finished tape from the recording studio and going straight to the meeting with the managing director of the new recording company. When he put the tape on his machine, there was not a note of music on it! He checked and re-checked the tape as he told us there definitely wasn't a fault in his tape recorder, until finally he gave up and telephoned the studio for a new tape. They said they would send it that afternoon – but, incredibly, the van bringing it broke down so he didn't get a copy till the next day. When he heard it at last, he decided to release it, hopefully before Christmas. We were then only six weeks away from that date yet somehow we just made it – despite the fact that, almost unsurprisingly now, there was a fault in the lacquer of the first pressing so it had to be done again.

Needless to say, promoting the record after all this was a risky business. On the first television we did, with Gloria Hunniford in Ulster Television, an arc-lamp above my head exploded approximately thirty seconds after I'd walked from under it, showering the spot with chunks of glass two inches thick. The lighting man told me it had never happened before in his studio experience. By this stage, it was impossible to explain all these things as coincidence, and I was becoming scared for the safety of all of us involved with the record. Damien and I prayed an awful lot during that time!

All in all, it's a very memorable record, and we really believe God has looked after us as even now peculiar things happen with this song. Just last year, for instance, I was guesting on a BBC radio show in Northern Ireland. They were coming back to the programme after the national news when suddenly there were panic stations. We were off the air!! Instead of the programme, listeners heard a two-minute silence! When I asked the DJ which track of my latest album he had been playing on the turn-table, it was hardly a surprise when he told me "Totus Tuus"!

The launching of "Totus Tuus" in December 1979 certainly caused more than a ripple. In Southern Ireland, it was received with huge enthusiasm and went to No. 1 within three weeks, and in January we were awarded a silver disc for 25,000 sales. But in Northern Ireland, I later learnt that it upset many people who felt that it was Catholic propaganda for the Pope. At the time, I really didn't realise this or I would have explained the reason and feelings behind the song in a much clearer way than perhaps I did. But despite all that went on, Damien and I were still keen to try and write more songs together and produced another six songs with a Christian theme. Turning over in our minds was the possibility of making an album of wholly Christian music, but the immediate problem was finding a company which would back such a commercial outsider.

In the meantime, several people had suggested that we release "Totus Tuus" in America. My manager at the time was the American, Jo Lustig, so we asked him whether he thought the idea was possible. "Not a hope," was his blunt reaction, and he went on to explain that the Christian market in America was controlled by the Southern Baptists who, according to Jo, would hardly want to handle a song inspired by the Pope's motto! The Christian company he suggested recording with was the famous Word label, but they, apparently, as staunch Baptists, wouldn't even look at me. Damien and I thought that was probably the end of the matter, but we prayed about it and left it with God.

Then, out of the blue, came a phone call from Susan in America. She had been contacted by Sam Sherrard, a minister friend of ours from Portadown, then living and working in Florida, who had told her of the huge National Religious Broadcasters' (NRB) conference which was being held in Washington in March. Sam felt sure that "Totus Tuus" ought to be heard there, but imagining that there was no way I would be able to come over, he had asked Susan to go and sing it. She in turn had rung my brother John to find out his reaction, and they both felt strongly that I should go over personally.

It seemed a mad idea, in view of what Jo had said, and I just didn't want to get involved. Damien had started his course at the rehabilitation centre in Dublin and I wanted to be at home with him. Besides, when I asked Jo for his opinion, he just replied, "You're crazy! If you just arrive unannounced and expect to be able to sing your little song, you'll be laughed out of the door." So I went back to Dublin, expecting Damien to agree how stupid it was, but, to my surprise, he said he felt I *should* go. My head really began to spin then. I talked with friends about it and one of them said to me that they had a feeling I would hear through a phone call what I should do. Well, I couldn't sit and wait for someone to call *me*, so I phoned up everyone I knew and asked what they thought I should do. I could hardly believe it when every single one replied, "I don't know, but we'll pray about it."

I was in awful confusion. John, meanwhile, had decided he would go out there anyway to have a scout round with Susan. Then, three days before he was due to fly, Damien's brother called round one Saturday morning as we were eating our breakfast and said nonchalantly, "You'll never guess who was on the phone to me yesterday. Father Thomas – from New York!" That made me nearly choke on my cornflakes because the last time I had heard, Father Thomas had been, as usual, in his enclosed community in Ireland. "Yes," Colm went on calmly, "he's looking forward to seeing you when you go out for the NRB conference."

It looked like I couldn't escape. I had to admit that this was the confirmation we had been waiting for, and soon I was on the plane to America with John, clutching just one cassette of "Totus Tuus" and one of "Praise the Lord" which we had to get copied as soon as we arrived. Although I could see no rhyme or reason for going, it was very obvious to me that the Lord wanted me to go there. This was my first experience of "stepping out in faith".

I'd never realised the size and importance of the event we were visiting, a gathering worthy of being opened by the US President, Mr Carter himself. Eight thousand religious broadcasters were there, and hundreds of famous names from the thriving Christian music scene in America. John, Susan and I trundled around wide-eyed like kids at a fair, feeling just a little bit conspicuous as it seemed there were only three Catholics there – us! I remembered what Jo Lustig had said and thought it might be a very good idea just to put our little cassettes in our pockets and go home. However, Susan and John had other ideas. They made an appointment to meet one of the organisers of the conference, a lovely Polish man who could hardly believe that we'd come all the way from Ireland without having arranged to meet anyone. I could hardly believe it myself – it seemed unreal, and all I could say was that I felt the Lord wanted me there. He was very kind to us, explaining as gently as possible that there was no possibility of my singing at the conference – something I'd realised the minute I'd walked through the door. I must admit, I felt very embarrassed when Susan told him I'd been in show business for ten years. At that moment I felt like a rank amateur. (A few years later I heard a nun called Mother Angelica talk of "making a fool of yourself for Christ" and I knew exactly what she meant!)

The day after we arrived, we met up with Sam Sherrard, and for the rest of the time we just wandered about, chatting to a few people without anyone showing particular interest in our material. Attention was all focussed on the really major artistes who performed each night, and on the final evening they all put on a huge concert which was televised nationally. One useful thing I did learn was that Word was definitely not the company for me, as they already had a very big star called Evie, and there was little hope of their taking on another girl of similar type. There was another apparently minor event which happened on the last day when we were introduced by Sam Sherrard to a lovely lady called Diane Bish, a very famous organist from Fort Lauderdale. She expressed an interest in my music and asked for a copy of each of the songs but didn't suggest she could do anything to promote them. We left the next day, seeing Father Thomas in New York on the way home, and feeling it had been a fascinating experience but one which seemed to close the door on any expansion in America.

Quite independently of all this, Damien and I had decided to go to the States that June for our holidays. Just before that, I was booked for some TV recordings in London. Suddenly there came another call from Susan. An American had been trying to contact me having been given Susan's number via Diane Bish. Susan had told him our address and also given him Dad's telephone number in London. Apparently this man, Kurt Kaiser, had written to me and tried phoning my father repeatedly but with no response. He had more or less given up when he found he had to go to London unexpectedly, and so in a last effort he contacted Susan again to say that if I could be reached he would be in a Mayfair hotel for a few days and would like to meet me there.

I knew no one of that name, and it all sounded very dubious to me. A complete stranger asking me to meet him in his hotel – the man might be a psychopath or something. (I don't need to tell you I have a very vivid imagination!) If I hadn't been going to London anyway I wouldn't have done anything about it, but as it was I decided it would probably be safe to arrange a brief meeting, and, being a dedicated coward, I took John and Gerald along with me. It seems so ridiculous looking back. Kurt Kaiser and his wife stepped out of the lift into the hotel foyer, and after five minutes it felt as if we'd known each other all our lives. There was an instant rapport. Kurt asked about my career and said he liked what he'd heard on tape, explaining that he was the vice-president of music with Word Records, though not suggesting that they were necessarily interested in recording me. We had a really lovely evening. They were just beautiful people and soon we were laughing and joking like old friends. Kurt and Pam had never been to Ireland and although, unfortunately, I had only four or five days in Ireland before flying to America, I asked them to come for a brief stay if they had the time.

To my surprise, they said they'd love to, and the following week they came to Moygannon for two days, striking a bargain with Damien and me that we should make a trip down to Waco, Texas, while we were in the States to meet some Word people. We flew out to America on the same day. Three weeks later, we found ourselves in *their* home – discovering just what a famous and talented man Kurt was as a producer and song-writer. One evening, he arranged a dinner party, and we were staggered to find that not only Gerald McCracken, the president of Word, but every member of the company's prestigious hierarchy had been invited too.

After the meal, Kurt casually suggested we did some singing

at the piano for the gathering. Not wanting to tread on any toes, I asked Kurt if he wanted "Praise the Lord". "No, I've never heard that one," he replied, "sing 'Totus Tuus'." I gulped, feeling a bit like a person putting their head in a noose, but I launched into it, trying to shut out what I imagined their expressions would be. I almost fell over moments later when, after the song, Gerald McCracken came over to me, took me by the hand, and pronounced like an Old Testament prophet, "That will be the first song you record for Word." And instantly I felt a voice inside saying just what Damien had insisted months back, "If the Lord wants it, it will happen."

The contract was signed soon after we came back to England. We sent off a whole tape of songs, some of which Damien and I had written, and Kurt sent me some music to look at, amongst which was a beautiful song he had written for me called "Sing for Me". An album to be called "Totally Yours" was discussed. The impossible was happening. The one song we felt would be the biggest barrier had proved the very bridge into the work we most wanted to do.

A year before, when we had felt I should be recording Christian songs, I'd had lots of doubts – not about my faith at all, but about finding material which really expressed what I believed and then finding the right company to release it. I had made an album for Warwick Records, a recording company which does a lot of TV advertising. "Twenty Inspirational Songs" had been released at Christmas 1980, but although we recorded some very fine songs, few of them really reflected my own experience. But Kurt's songs were completely different. Here was something that seemed exactly to express my own situation and beliefs. I could completely identify with what I was singing about, and it revolutionised my attitude towards contemporary Christian music. There had been so many confirmations along the way that I was sure now it was right to work in this field, and my faith had grown through all that had happened so that it didn't feel so strange singing directly about God and my beliefs.

Life was changing direction in more ways than one. That

The birth of Grace: four generations.

Dancing in a TV Christmas special.

Wedding Day, October 5th 1978.

Relaxation on a bicycle.

summer we discovered to our joy that I was pregnant. I remember vividly the day I was told. It was a beautiful sunny afternoon and we were sitting in the garden, waiting for the doctor to ring with the results of my test. Each time the phone rang my heart stopped – then finally came the call we were waiting for.

We both wanted children and we were very excited and happy about the news. I remember thinking that I didn't look or physically feel any different (luckily I didn't suffer from morning sickness) so I really found it hard to believe that I was carrying a child. It was almost as though it was happening to someone else. I must say too that although I was delighted, I was also nervous, even frightened at the thought of being a parent. What kind of mother would I make? Thankfully, Damien and I were able to talk openly about the fears we both shared and that really helped.

Our baby was due in January 1981 and as Damien was to take his final exams in Dublin in December 1980 we knew the time was right for us to sit down and really think about what course we wanted our life to take as a family. Both of us felt that a new phase was about to open in my music career, but we were equally convinced that children should never come second to my work. So the best solution seemed to be to do as much work as possible while they were young enough to travel with us, and we decided that when his course was finished Damien would do more on the business side of my work so that we could be together.

Around this time, I was offered the opportunity of doing a whole summer season in Torquay the following year. From a personal and financial point of view, it was impossible to refuse, and that marked my very conscious decision to return to work. I certainly had the energy for it. After a few initial weeks of feeling very tired but not sick, I took on the classic pregnancy "bloom". My hair shone, my skin cleared and I felt wonderful. I still couldn't fully believe the miracle of what was happening inside me, but the baby became very real and very precious to me after a threatened miscarriage at two months. I was over in England when it happened so it was a couple of days before I was able to get to my obstetrician in Ireland. By then, I was convinced I had lost the baby, but when he did a scan he pointed to a vague blob on the screen and assured me that there was the embryo safe and sound. It jarred on me to hear it called an "embryo" as the two days' delay in seeing him had developed in me a desperate need to keep the baby and seeing it on the scan had brought it home to me that this was a real child and not just a splurge of cells. After that, I had two more scans and as we watched it grow, it became more and more real to us. We prayed together for the baby each day, asking the Lord to protect our child and fill it with His Holy Spirit. We talked to it and told it that we loved it too, because we both felt that even in the womb a baby can be susceptible to insecurity and rejection. Right from the beginning I think it's important that the baby is surrounded by an atmosphere of love where it feels wanted and secure.

In fact that was how the song "Little Baby" from the album "Totally Yours" came to be written. After the great relief of being told that I hadn't miscarried it suddenly dawned on me that for two months I'd ignored my child completely. Now I had a real need to talk to my baby and let it know that I loved and wanted it very much – so I thought, what's the best way to talk to a baby? I decided that I should sing it a little lullaby. At once I had the words:

Little baby yet unborn
In my womb so safe and warm
Living with me who will you be?
Living with me I wish I could see
My little baby yet unborn
In my womb so safe and warm.

I ended up singing that for weeks – until I sang it for Damien, then together we thought of the things we wanted to tell our child. One thing in particular was that if he or she were handicapped in any way, not to worry, we would still love and want them. So the verse was written:

> If you laugh or if you cry
> I'm gonna love you till I die
> Living with me you always will be
> Living with me and so it shall be
> If you laugh or if you cry
> I'm gonna love you till I die.

It started out as Grace's song. It's now become Ruth and John-James's song too!

Our "Little Baby" entered the world on January 18th 1981 after an emergency Caesarean – not quite the natural birth I had imagined. The baby was a week overdue so I was induced, but by five in the morning, after eighteen hours of labour, I was exhausted, and the medical staff were afraid the baby was getting distressed. It became obvious I had to have a Caesarean. Damien was fantastic all through my labour, and I found it invaluable to have him there. When I came round from the operation there he was, telling me we had a beautiful little girl. I just stared at this little bundle in the cot beside my bed – and prayed she wouldn't move or wake up. I felt so tired. Empty. Somehow I couldn't see Grace as my own child, just a little baby, any baby. I felt like I'd missed the birth! The relationship I'd built up with her in the womb seemed to have disappeared into thin air, and it took me some days to see her individual personality, and to feel warmth and love inside. For the first few weeks, I struggled with feelings of depression, guilty about my lack of enthusiasm and frustrated by the overwhelming sense of tiredness, until finally I was able to accept my reaction as quite normal and see that I hadn't "failed" somehow by not giving birth naturally.

Despite the emptiness I sometimes felt, I was determined to work at establishing that closeness, the bonding, I had imagined I would have with my baby. I had always wanted to feed Grace myself and this I did for twelve weeks until pressure of work made it impossible to go on. As the weeks went by, I felt closer and closer to her. But at times it wasn't easy. Grace cried and cried, often curling up with dreadful colic, and I just didn't know what to do. It took me some while to learn to trust my instincts as to whether she was ill or hungry, dirty or bored, and at first I used to ask everyone's advice and still feel just as unsure. But as my confidence increased I relaxed and was able to experience that close and loving relationship I wanted with our beautiful little daughter.

With sleepless nights because of Grace, and weeks spent working on our first Christian album with Word, Damien and I felt pretty shattered during the spring, but it was still with a sense of peace and satisfaction that we saw "Totally Yours" finally recorded in April. Then straight away we were heading off to Torquay for our summer season.

Even though I was so tired, I was really glad for Grace's sake that we would be able to stay in one place for five months. We rented a beautiful house on top of a hill overlooking a wooded valley. From our living room we could see the sea, glinting in the sunshine, and when the wind was in the right direction you could smell the sharp salt tang of the waves and hear the wailing cry of the seagulls in the harbour. Up until then, my mother and grandmother, or our faithful friend Bridie, the ex-housekeeper from Damien's hotel, had travelled with us to help out with Grace, but now we found a temporary nanny to live in. Life couldn't have seemed more comfortable. Yet there was one thing I was really worried about. My voice.

I hadn't done a season since my throat operation, and most of the work I'd been involved in recently had been recorded, not live. I'd been seeing Florence Norberg regularly, and she seemed able to pick me up from the depths of depression about my voice, and inspire me with confidence. It was incredible the results her methods had achieved so that even when my throat felt like a cheese-grater, she could draw out a beautiful sound. But down in Devon, miles from her encouragement, I worried myself into a panic in a few days. Exhausted and tense, I was convinced that my throat was closing up so that

I could hardly get a sound out, and on top of that, my heart seemed to be having palpitations.

Miserably, I presented myself at the local GP's surgery in Torquay, sure that I was sickening for some terrible virus or other. But Dr Jack, an eccentric, absent-minded professor type straight out of Dickens, had no time for viruses. Sweeping aside my muttered explanations, he slapped the desk and cried, "Nerves, my girl," and reaching up to the top of his heavy Victorian bookshelf, he took down a weighty medical volume and read out an exact description of my symptoms. Briskly, but kindly, he explained that my only problem was nervous hysteria, and assured me that as far as he could see there was nothing at all wrong with my throat. All my worries seemed to evaporate, and soon I found myself laughing for the first time in days as he told me funny stories about another singer he had treated.

Dr Jack kept an expert fatherly eye on me for the whole of the season, but I never had any trouble with my voice after that, except for the effects of tiredness which I had learnt to overcome by Florence Norberg's method. In every other way, the season was a joy to do. I was appearing in two performances a day with Peter Goodwright and Arthur Worsley who, with their wives, became very close friends of ours. We were like one big family in a wonderfully relaxed and successful season. In August there was some ruction at the new theatre in Paignton where another show had been running, and we were asked to transfer our show to the Princess Theatre there. That meant two opening nights in one season which could have been quite a strain, but everything seemed to flow along smoothly until we closed on October 5th.

The long season hadn't done much for my tiredness, though, so in the autumn we went on holiday with my parents to Florida for three weeks. Grace distinguished herself by not sleeping a wink for the whole of the nine-hour flight, and bouncing up and down on my knees so that I was black and blue by the time we arrived, but after that, she enchanted everyone for the whole holiday. At ten months, she was crawling like a human dodgem, but she hated stones, and if the ground was uneven she developed an extraordinary way of crawling on tiptoe which captivated everyone. But with her thick blonde curls and wide smile, she could have melted the hardest heart anyway.

America was a great rest, but just too short. The pressure piled on as soon as we got back with most of the winter spent travelling in Europe doing TV work. Damien came too, but this time it seemed less unsettling for Grace to leave her in London with my mother and father. Grace was fine while we were away, but when we came back she couldn't leave me for a moment, and went through a very "clinging" stage. I wanted desperately to re-establish her sense of security, but life was hectic all through the spring of 1982 during which I recorded a new secular album called "Magic". Then I was launched straight into an eighteen-week summer season of two shows a day in Blackpool with Little and Large. It was great to be in one place again, and I could spend the mornings with Grace, though I could never bath her and put her to bed, never enjoy that special time for stories and cuddles that can create such a bond between mother and child. Straight after the summer season which was a wonderful success, one of the top three shows in England, we went off to Portugal for some TV work and took Grace with us.

By September I was beginning to feel like I was on a helter-skelter. There seemed to be no time to relax as a family – in fact no time to relax at all – yet I felt locked into the situation and I was beginning to feel I had no control over my own life. I had thought we would have plenty of time together over the winter, but now I found that my diary was fully booked with European engagements and television work.

On top of this, I had another major commitment – the release of our second album with Word, "Let There Be Light", a medley of widely different styles from up-tempo numbers through jazz to a lovely old Irish hymn which I sang in Gaelic. My feet never seemed to touch the ground, and I felt that our family was just being swept along by events so that we were losing our identity as a unit. I was constantly worrying about not spending enough time with the family and experiencing awful guilt when I had to be away, so that I was often in tears. I used to look at Grace and feel she was in a glass case and I couldn't reach her. At last, in desperation, we prayed that God would use any means to get us back on sure ground as a family.

He wasn't long in answering, though at first it looked as if He hadn't heard. I was booked to do a pantomime in Hull over Christmas, and that in itself went really well, but Grace was very ill for the whole of the time with ear infections and raging temperatures. Poor Bridie was looking after us again and I think she was more exhausted than any of us, though she remained a tower of strength right through. The cast of the panto were a lovely bunch of people, but I couldn't enjoy it to the full as I felt so worn out. Then, to crown it all, I seemed to catch some sort of tummy bug. The musical director, and comedian Mike Newman, also went down with it, but when I was still feeling ill after Christmas I began to wonder if there wasn't another reason. Eventually, I went to see the doctor. He sent me to the obstetrician! On January 6th I learnt I was expecting another baby.

13

It was really the last thing I'd have thought of, yet I felt it was an answer to my prayers. Automatically, certain commitments for 1983 had to be cancelled, and we all knew that there would definitely be a time of being at home all together as a family during the summer and autumn. What we could see we desperately needed, though, was a permanent nanny to help provide stability and continuity for the children, and to bale us out in the growing demands of domestic life. We found someone who has been an invaluable member of our family ever since.

Sue Sheard had been a student at Endsleigh College of Higher Education in Hull. After qualifying there as a PE teacher she not only taught in a girls' private school in Richmond, North Yorkshire, but also worked as an auxiliary geriatric nurse in Leeds and did some general nursing in London. While we were in Hull, I met the Principal of Endsleigh College. She was a lovely, gentle person, and I found myself pouring out all our problems about finding the right person to look after Grace and the coming baby. She promised to help if she could. A few days later she phoned to say that one of her ex-pupils had come to visit her. It was Sue – apparently she was very unhappy in her present job and as Mother Agnes thought she could be very suitable for us, she suggested that we meet. I wasn't very hopeful as she seemed if anything overqualified for our needs. When we met I told her all the bad things about our lifestyle so that she'd be under no illusions about a glamorous life. Later she told me that she herself had been dubious as to whether the job was suitable from her point of view, but right from the beginning we just clicked. I knew she could fit into our family and with her unique Yorkshire blend of common sense and a lively sense of humour, she obviously felt she could identify with our aims and values, as well as our humdrum routine. Turning down a plum teaching job, she joined us in March – and life has never been the same since. With her unflagging hard work, efficiency and patience, she helps banish the chaos and provides a constant atmosphere of loving order and capability which Damien and I appreciate as much as the children.

On February 5th we left Hull and the following month we went off to America with Grace and Sue for a much-needed holiday, as I hadn't had three days off in a row for about two years. Coming back, we moved into a flat in London, just ten minutes' drive from the centre, so that we didn't waste time travelling and life could be more relaxing and settled when we were working in England. I did some TV work at the end of April, but the summer season that had been arranged with the Delfont Organisation had to be cancelled because of the forthcoming baby. Around this time, the publishers approached me with the idea of this book, and again, the timing seemed just right as I had reached a point in my career where the various aspects of my life had reached a balance, perhaps a maturity, which enabled me to take stock of my situation, and talk more clearly about the way ahead – plus the fact that for the first time in ages it looked as though I would have time to sit down and actually think. But there was still some travelling to be done before that was possible.

In the middle of June, I flew to Germany to do a TV show, but the producer was horrified when he saw my blossoming tum! Well, I *was* seven months pregnant so it was very difficult to hide this light under a bushel. The show was a 6.30 p.m. family slot, but the producer insisted that it wasn't attractive or decent to allow me to appear in my condition. I don't often get angry, but such a narrow-minded attitude really did annoy me. Eventually he compromised by producing an enormous bunch of flowers, ordering me to hold them in front of me and not to move! I'm glad to say that this is the only time I have been confronted with this attitude. People are more often very encouraging and thoughtful.

Straight after this, Damien, Grace and I went to Donegal for a quiet week together. We had a lovely break there, a special time to talk and think and pray. My last trip before Ruth's birth was by air to Washington DC for the Christian Booksellers' Conference where I was to promote my two Christian albums.

At this stage I was eight months pregnant, and as we got on the plane I could see the stewardess eyeing me worriedly. All through the flight she kept glancing at me nervously, and eventually she came over and asked me when the baby was due.

"In about three or four weeks," I said cheerfully, "but don't worry. You must have done a course on emergency delivery."

"Yes, I did," she admitted, "but I felt ill watching the film so I never saw the end!"

Luckily she wasn't called to witness it on that flight, and I bet she prayed she wouldn't be on duty when I took the flight home.

The conference in Washington was a fascinating experience, and we met some really interesting and lovely people from the Christian book and music worlds, not to mention our dear friends Kurt and Pat Kaiser and a second meeting with Diane Bish. The only thing weighing on my mind was the prospect of the birth I was going back to. After the Caesarean with Grace, I wanted very much to be able to have this baby naturally. Apart from anything else, I was scheduled to be back at work, slim and fit, within ten weeks. The closer the birth got, the more I worried, although I didn't mention my worries to anyone but Damien. Then one day I was sitting in a booth at the conference signing copies of the album "Totally Yours" as people filed past. Suddenly I felt a gentle hand on mine, and I looked up into the face of a stranger, a woman.

Before I could do more than smile hello, she was saying, "Don't worry. Everything is going to be all right – you will have a natural childbirth." Then she was swallowed up in the crowd.

I'd never seen this woman before in my life, and she couldn't possibly have known my secret fear. To me this was another example of how the Lord speaks to us through discerning people and it was a big encouragement, a sort of promise which I tried to cling to in the next few weeks. The return flight went safely, though it was amusing to find Heathrow Airport at 7.30 a.m. swarming with reporters and photographers waiting to see me. Apparently, while I'd been away, news had come of some poor woman giving birth on a jumbo jet from Australia, and the press were dying to see whether I had made it or not. It seemed almost a shame to disappoint them.

My baby was due on August 12th. I felt heavy and uncomfortable in the hot weather, and I hoped I wouldn't go over that date. But at my final examination, the doctor's verdict was that it would be overdue. I tried not to give way to the feeling of panic that this was the same pattern as the last time, but when I went for another check-up on the 15th, I was told that there was still no change. I left in tears. That was Monday. Damien and I sat down and really prayed that I'd be able to hand this over to the Lord. He knew what was best for my baby and for me. However, if possible, could He speed things up a bit?

I felt a lot happier and relaxed after that and I had the comfort too of knowing that round the world our friends were also praying for us. Then on Wednesday afternoon, I hardly dared believe that the mild contractions I was feeling were the real thing. We had been invited to supper with Mary, Damien's sister, who lived quite near us and I sat down that evening to the biggest meal I think I've ever eaten. The pains were very erratic and I didn't want to make a fuss if it was a false alarm, so I surreptitiously wrote down the intervals between the contractions on a piece of paper under the tablecloth. By midnight we decided I'd better pack my bag. I lay down for a while and the contractions began to come more rapidly, so at 3.30 a.m. Damien and I were arriving at Daisy Hill Hospital in Newry. Four hours later Suzanna Ruth made her calm, uncomplicated entry into the world. The hospital staff were wonderful. Damien and I were over the moon and I thanked God that everything had gone so smoothly. The woman's prophecy in America had come true. It had meant so much to us to have the baby naturally with Damien at my side right the way through, and the first few weeks seemed almost peaceful in comparison with how I felt after Grace's birth. Grace was fascinated by her little sister who, right from the beginning, has been a really sunny, contented wee thing.

I was able to feed her for about eight weeks but then work commitments began to crowd in once again and regretfully I had to stop. But during these weeks I found such peace being at the hub of the family once more, and we all enjoyed the first semblance of routine in our domestic life for ages – as much routine as a new baby allows, that is! There was such pleasure in simple things like family meals, being able to bath the children and tuck them up in bed and then to sit down together for a peaceful moment at the end of the day. But Christmas was almost upon us – and that meant pantomime!

It had always been my ambition to do a season in the West End. There is a special sense of community in the West End theatre and I'd heard people talk about the magic of being part of that excitement and atmosphere. At last my chance had come. The previous year's panto in Hull had been so successful that it was transferred to the West End with the same cast and I found it was true about the magic, especially as we were in the theatre where all Nöel Coward's plays had been staged, someone of whom I'm a big fan. There were pictures of him everywhere and in fact I was using his dressing room. I would sit there at times and imagine him lounging on the settee or making-up in front of the mirror. It was a theatre full of colour and atmosphere and I have very happy memories of our seven-week run there. In fact it was so successful (on one particular weekend, we had the biggest box-office sales in the whole of the West End) that the show was extended for another five weeks though unfortunately I had other engagements booked and couldn't stay on.

I always enjoy doing pantomime. There is a special satisfaction playing to children. Every night their excitement and wonder makes the show come alive and the cast finds itself responding to each audience in a different way with new ad libs. Children's enthusiasm is so infectious and I love their lack of inhibition. We have a lovely story of the night when Snow White (me) was about to take a bite of the poisoned apple. The boys and girls were in a frenzy, jumping up and down, screaming and shouting – but one little boy of about six was particularly noticeable as he hung over the orchestra waving his arms for attention and shouting at the top of his voice, "Don't eat it – it's poisoned, it's poisoned!" This went on for quite a few minutes during which the little fellow got more and more agitated and shouted all the louder, "Don't eat it – it's poisoned." Suddenly the fateful bite was taken and as Snow White collapsed dramatically there was a stunned silence over the auditorium – except for the little boy who announced for all to hear, "You stupid thing, I *told* you not to eat it!" A second later the whole theatre including a "dead" Snow White were rocking with laughter.

Apart from the panto, I was doing lots of "televisions" around that time, along with endless promotion and press interviews, but one engagement, at least, didn't take me away from the family. That Christmas, the whole lot of us, including Sue and Damien's brother Gerald, appeared on TV-AM's Christmas Day Special. What a day that was. I don't think any of us got a wink of sleep the night before as we sat up chatting and opening presents until the small hours and had to leave for the studios at five thirty in the morning. We all enjoyed it though Grace proved herself a natural performer, and ended up trying to bottle-feed Rusty Lee's baby boy. As for Damien, he's never been an extrovert and was only too glad for the show to be stolen by his bright-as-a-button eldest daughter and a smiling, gurgling (and occasionally burping) Ruth who was dressed in a pink tracksuit and tiny leg-warmers, much to the delight of Wincy Willis and Anne Diamond!

There was no let-up in the pressure of work during the spring, mostly the same round of recordings and media interviews, plus a big concert in the Albert Hall in aid of the RSPB, attended by Princess Margaret (at which one of the stars went on stage in a feather boa!). A hectic schedule wasn't unusual, but something which did puzzle us was the number of things which seemed to go wrong. Obviously show-business is an unpredictable world, but around this time it seemed as though a problem arose in nearly everything we did. In the middle of everything, Florence Norberg died suddenly, having secretly suffered from cancer and other illnesses for some time, and I said goodbye at the hospital to a much loved and needed friend. She is one of those irreplaceable people that you're blessed to meet in life and I'll never forget the love and support she gave me. Then, around the same time, Grace became ill with terrible tummy pains which landed her in hospital for tests. I was just about to begin filming a TV special, but between sitting up with her in hospital through the night and feeling worried and guilty when I couldn't be with her through the day, my special was the last thing on my mind.

Damien and I were just worn out and eventually we decided that all these problems happening at the same time had to be more than just coincidences. Then we realised we were just a few weeks away from an American tour of Christian concerts and appearances on most of the national religious TV and radio shows. We had felt for some time that this tour was going to be a very significant one for us although it had been pushed into the background by all that was going on – to be truthful by this time I didn't want to be away from home in case something else went wrong. However, we could see that this was a similar pattern to previous times when I'd been involved in Christian work, so I decided to put it in the Lord's hands and try to carry on with the agreed plans. Once I did that I felt calmer and more in control. To our great relief, the results of Grace's tests showed there was nothing wrong and thankfully her pains subsided. As the day of our departure neared, I still dreaded the thought of leaving her and Ruth. I know that if I'd been going to America to sing on a solely commercial basis I'd probably have felt like cancelling everything, but I felt that I was really intended to go there.

In my limited experience, I had already discovered how God could move and speak to people through my songs without my realising it. We can all be instruments of God's grace and blessing if we make our ability and our time available to Him. Sometimes people come up to me after a concert and say how one of the songs perhaps has really made them see that God loves them or has given them a new sense of direction and peace. I get letters, too, from people who have found a deeper relationship with the Lord through listening to one of my Christian albums or have found the courage to be more open about their faith after hearing me talk about my relationship with God in some interview or article.

It still amazes me that I was given the freedom and the courage to be able to share my very deepest feelings – but I know too that, as I've said before, every time I'm involved in Christian work, I come up against tremendous opposition. Now I don't mean there's a little red devil with a tail, hopping up and down in a rage brandishing a pitchfork. But it stands to reason that if you accept that there is a force for Good, you must accept there is a force for Evil. Most of us aren't really aware of this evil force because, as people say, the devil doesn't bother you until you bother him. It can't make him very happy if you come into a new personal relationship with God, and particularly if you start trying to share that peace and joy. I don't mean to sound glib though. Spiritual attack is a very real thing, and if you don't understand what's happening you can feel confused and depressed. But the wonderful thing is that the Lord gives you the strength to deal with these difficult times. In fact, it seems as though it's often through these trials that we experience the greatest blessing and the reality of God's power. It is working through these periods of difficulty, depending solely on the Lord for strength and direction, that we grow as people and in our spiritual relationship with Him and are able to understand and help other people going through similar difficulties.

Well, our departure day arrived and for some mysterious reason, the jet in which we flew to the States shed bits of debris as we passed over Reading and eventually had to make an emergency landing back at Heathrow airport. That was a frightening experience though no one was hurt and I don't think most of us realised quite how serious the situation was. Still, we understood all this spiritual opposition when we got to America.

It was an exhausting programme but very enjoyable. With Kurt Kaiser, I sang in churches of every denomination and concert halls all over the States, and did endless television and radio shows.

Everywhere we went, it was wonderful for us to meet new people with such a love of the Lord both in the churches and in the media and music world. The "family of God" really does exist. I sang in a variety of places, from huge auditoriums right down to one occasion when we visited a tiny church in the Bayou or swamp country near New Orleans. In this little village, the whole community came out led by Father Rock, a priest of Red Indian descent who brought his mother, aged ninety. She sat dignified and still in the front row, a beautiful old lady with the high Indian cheekbones and a skin like wrinkled leather. She couldn't speak a word of English but her son assured us that she enjoyed the music.

I also sang at a college in Alabama – where we experienced the worst electrical storm we'd ever known. It was the night before we left America and we were staying in the home of the dean of the college. The air was very stuffy and hot and we had the windows thrown open wide as we did some last-minute packing. It was the tornado season, and we listened uneasily as the wind gradually picked up and began to blow in thick, hot gusts through the windows. Suddenly there was a blinding flash of light and almost simultaneously a violent crash of thunder which sounded like an earthquake and shook the whole house. I've never moved so fast. In a second Damien and I had leapt over the suitcase, run out of the door and were shaking like jellies in the corridor. Our first thought was to see that Kurt was all right, but when we turned towards his room, we saw that his light was out and assumed that somehow he was managing to sleep through it all. The storm buffeted the house for some time but slowly moved away and eventually we crawled warily back to bed. The next morning, the tap-water was rust-coloured and we were told that the lightning had actually struck the house. Amazed at Kurt's apparent oblivion during the night, we asked him if he had heard anything.

"*Heard* anything?" he exclaimed. "I think the lightning must have hit my room. It sounded like an explosion and my light went out. I was so terrified that I dived under the bedclothes and prayed for someone to come. I didn't get a wink of sleep all night." Damien and I laughed as we told him of the two of us cowering with fear outside Kurt's door, envying his peaceful sleep.

This American tour added many good friends to the ones we already had in the States. I'd already had the privilege of meeting Billy Graham when I had been invited to sing on three nights at his New England Crusade in Boston in the spring of 1982. I had been curious, perhaps even a bit sceptical, about what sort of a man Billy Graham was, but when I heard him speak I was very impressed. When he preaches it is with a power and conviction that just couldn't be fake. As an entertainer, I'm aware of how it is possible to manipulate an audience from the stage, but Billy Graham used no tricks at all. Everything he said was with utter sincerity and simplicity. I was honoured – if a bit scared – that he asked me to say something about myself and my faith before I sang. Being aware of the sad suspicions some people have about Catholics being Christians, I didn't mention what denomination I came from, but afterwards Dr Graham specifically asked me to say that I was a Catholic on the following night, and I must say that the reaction of the people was warm and receptive. In fact, as a result of that I was asked to take part in Billy Graham's Mission England in 1984.

But unknown to almost everyone I had a secret worry which was making my spirits sink lower and lower. It had its roots ten years ago. I've never wanted to know the future. Oh, I was curious about it and like most people I'd sometimes read my daily horoscope for fun but I would never go to fortune-tellers of any kind because I felt nervous of anyone telling me what was going to happen in my life. Of course now I believe God has got a plan for our lives and all we need to do is live a day at a time. But in 1974 I was doing some concerts in Scotland when I happened to meet a girl who had been able to foresee the future right from a little child. She had been brought up a member of the Plymouth Brethren church but had been told to leave by the elders because they felt her gift wasn't from God. This girl had a friend with her and as we were chatting the other girl said, "Why don't you let her tell you something of your life." Because I hadn't gone to this girl myself it didn't immediately strike me that this was just the same as visiting a fortune-teller. Curiosity got the better of me and she proceeded to tell me all sorts of things about my future. Many of them turned out to be true – she told me I would marry Damien, for instance, long before there was any talk of that between us. She also told me I would have two children. I didn't think any more of it until Ruth was born and then I suddenly remembered her words. I had always wanted a large family, but now I felt that because she'd been right in other things she must be right in this point too and that I wouldn't be able to have another child. It seemed so ridiculous that I couldn't even tell Damien about it but it got to the point where I felt so worried and depressed I kept breaking into tears and eventually out the story came. It was such a relief to be able to tell someone and to be reassured that God was in control of my life and whatever was *His* will for me would happen. I really prayed that I would be able to have another child. I wasn't sure whether I was more shocked or pleased when I discovered I was pregnant only a few weeks later! Ruth was only seven months old at that time.

The battle wasn't over though. I then began to have terrible thoughts that I would miscarry or the baby would be born dead. Normally when I pray about something, I feel peaceful that it is in God's hands. But with this I just couldn't shake off the feeling of doom. It dogged me all the way through pregnancy, which went perfectly smoothly, and even after the straightforward birth of a beautiful son I couldn't get rid of this nagging fear. Unbelievably I then became convinced that something would happen to Grace or Ruth. It wasn't until we all got down as a family and prayed for that curse to be broken, and that my fear of what she'd told me would be lifted that I really felt free at last. Now I know why Christians always said fortune-telling was wrong. Most of us have a great curiosity about the future, and fortune-telling can cash in on our hopes and fears. It may tell you a lot of truths but it can rob you of your peace and I believe that to put the direction of your life in anyone but the Lord's hands is extremely dangerous.

I don't know if my manager groaned when he heard I was pregnant again but in fact we didn't have to make really major changes in our schedule. I went ahead with the summer season already booked at Great Yarmouth, and once again enjoyed the luxury of being together as a family for several months. I had two shows a day, afternoon and evening, so I was able to spend the mornings with the children making sandcastles on the beach and going for walks together.

In fact, we really felt the Lord was looking after us there right from the beginning. In the weeks before the start of the shows, we drew a complete blank trying to find accommodation for the season. Four bedroomed houses to let didn't seem to exist. We had been told the most pleasant area to stay but everyone shook their heads at the chances of finding anything vacant there at this stage. With just four days to go, we were relatively calm, holding on firmly to the belief that the Lord did have the right house for us, even if He was a bit slow in letting us know about it. Damien went off to Great Yarmouth for one last try. He had only one house to view and it turned out to be unsuitable. The next morning before leaving he rang the estate agent again, who said another house had suddenly become available. Reluctantly he went to view it, expecting the worst – only to discover it was exactly right for us in every way and it was situated in the beautiful area we'd been told about. It was quickly settled and we moved straight in. Coming from the flat in busy central London we found the house perfect. It was situated down a private residential road just three minutes from the beach. It also had an enclosed garden at the back so for the children (and us!) it was paradise.

An added blessing was that we found a lovely obstetrician just two streets down from where we were living. We'd really been praying that we would find someone good and kind, particularly as I still had these nagging fears about the pregnancy despite feeling extremely fit. The first time I visited his surgery, my eye was caught by a Christian magazine on the table at reception and I soon discovered that Mr Breeze and his wife had both been missionaries. They were a lovely Christian couple and became good friends, looking after me wonderfully during our time there. I kept very well except for picking up a virus which forced me to take three days off in the middle of the season. Actually it was the rest of the family which had a bad time healthwise, causing us a lot of concern, though, again, we found the Lord gave us peace and strength even when Grace got viral pneumonia. We had tremendous support from the other artists in the show – like Tom O'Connor, and my good friends Les Dennis and Dustin Gee – who used to tease me unmercifully about my ever-increasing "bump". Bella Emberg was also on the bill (she plays Blunderwoman in *Russ Abbot's Madhouse* on ITV). I don't think she'd mind being called a very "big lady." We used to joke that by the end of the season, no one would be able to tell the difference between us!

All through this period, though, there was one large blot on our happiness. My father was very ill, as indeed he had been for some time. God had already done such wonderful things in Dad's life. After three coronaries and open heart surgery between 1976 and 1983, he'd been prayed for many times without any dramatic physical healing. But then, in May 1983, we held a healing Mass for him in London where Sister Breige McKenna and Father Kevin laid hands on him and prayed that the Lord would give him a new heart. At this time Dad couldn't walk any distance without severe pain and shortness of breath. In fact he was in constant pain. Soon after that Mass the pain disappeared, and he found he was able to walk up and down the hill to the shops with little effort. So he stopped taking most of his tablets. (He had been on about forty a day.) Incredibly, although X-rays showed that his heart appeared to be the same, the symptoms had vanished. That June he flew to America to stay with Susan for three months and was up every morning at seven and working the fields in a tractor until sundown.

Back home, though, the following spring, circulation problems in his legs began to worsen. His doctor knew for some time that he needed surgery on his legs but was afraid to do anything because of his heart condition. Then, in the summer of 1984, he was rushed into hospital where they discovered he had the beginnings of gangrene in his foot. It was a terrible shock to us all and he has suffered a great deal since then both in physical pain and mental anguish.

I can honestly say that I've never known such a brave man. Even in his worst moments he'll try to crack a joke. We've all seen how his relationship with the Lord has deepened and grown, and also how the Lord has worked very obviously in his life and in my mother's. Through three major operations – including the amputation of his leg – his heart, as the surgeon put it, took it all with "the ease of someone taking a cup of tea". He spends hours in prayers, sometimes the whole of those long sleepless nights of pain. But it hasn't been an easy time for him. The strength to fight on has often been difficult to find. But not long ago, when he was going through a very difficult period, a complete stranger came to my parents' door. He had been told about my father and had come to see him because he himself had suffered from exactly the same medical condition and yet had experienced a wonderful healing. My parents were staggered. At last, here was someone who really understood the pain my father was suffering and yet could talk positively about God's power to heal and about the need to keep hoping. Since then he has come to talk and pray with my father almost every day. As soon as anyone meets Dad now they talk of the atmosphere of peace about him and it's just beautiful to see the way he is trusting the Lord now for strength and healing. And of course what has happened has had a deep healing effect on the whole of my family. We have always been a close family, but now there is an even deeper love and trust between us.

Before our third baby was born, we managed to grab a week's holiday at the end of October, armed with a letter from my obstetrician to say I was allowed to fly as I was now eight and a half months pregnant and extremely large! We just made it back in time and John-James Robert was born at the Westminster Hospital on November 5th. In fact, just as he was delivered, fireworks started to go off all over London; quite a dramatic entrance to the world.

Again, the weeks surrounding the birth were an oasis. John-James was such an easy baby (a real answer to prayer, I'm sure). I was able to feed him for five weeks and then I had to start rehearsals for panto in Wolverhampton – the most buxom Snow White that ever trod the boards.

In some ways, show business is like school; work seems divided into terms which themselves follow the seasons. This ever-revolving pattern of events could be seen as boring and repetitive, and some people I speak to view it as the very opposite of the glamorous, glitzy world others imagine. The truth is somewhere in between, of course. The cycle of summer seasons and pantomimes, television and radio shows, promotions and tours sometimes seems a grind, but there is also a certain security and stability about it, plus the real pleasure of meeting up with old friends at different venues (like rejoining old classmates after the break of the summer holidays). This pattern of life, which can produce terrible loneliness and put great strain on relationships and families, can also provide a sense of identity and belonging if you stick it out long enough.

Comparatively, there aren't that many people earning a living from show business, and in a sense it is like an exclusive club – great if you're a "member", but grim if you're always floating alone on the outside.

I'm beginning to find my arithmetic a bit shaky when I try to add up how many years I've been in entertainment, but personally I find the wheel of life in show business like a carousel at a fair, revolving on the same axis, but offering different seats and changing views and pleasures at every turn. For the past few years, for example, I have found myself appearing as Snow White in Christmas pantomimes. I am threatened that I'll have to go on doing it "until you get it right!". The script may be pretty much the same, even down to the jokes, and I might be working with much the same cast as previous seasons, but somehow there is still a freshness about almost every performance. No two audiences respond in the same way, and the sense of satisfaction you feel from their pleasure and excitement is a boost every time. There are many jobs where you could slog away for days without the reward of any obvious signs of achievement or success. And working with people (especially children quite often) means there is always the unexpected, including the mistakes, to bring interest and colour to the routine.

It's fun, too, exploring different parts of the country, not to mention travelling abroad, though I wouldn't do it if it weren't possible for the children to come as well most of the time. In the summer of 1985 we went to Bournemouth where we were fortunate to rent a beautiful house. With just one show every evening, I was able to spend all day with the family, and that is a privilege for any parent (though some might not agree!). One or two vivid memories of that summer stick in my mind. At the end of the season, the whole cast had a water polo match which was hilarious for those who couldn't really swim let alone play water polo. And at church one Sunday, Grace suddenly shrieked, "Chitty Chitty Bang Bang!" which couldn't be passed off as one of the liturgical responses. She had spotted Lionel Jeffries, the famous actor who played the father in our children's favourite film. But a less enjoyable episode was going down with salmonella poisoning, which made me very ill for quite a while, though at least I lost nearly a stone in weight. In fact the dancers in the cast suggested I bottle the virus!

My next project in the autumn was the making of a video of one of my fifties singles, "If I Gave My Heart For You". It was great fun. We took over a wonderfully authentic period ballroom and spent from dawn till midnight filming, with everyone getting into the spirit of the times. Even my hairdresser, Simon, took up the part of the barman. Perhaps he couldn't wait to get at the grease pot to stick his hair down. At the end of it all, we descended on the little corner cafe in the street and ordered egg and chips for about forty! The few other customers enjoying a late night romantic fry-up à deux thought it was a teddy-boy take-over.

Snow White in Newcastle brought together the old team, I was back working with my friend Mike Newman. It was three years since we had worked together but it all clicked straight away and the show was a great success, breaking all box office records for that theatre. The only shadow over that time was the early death of a very dear and talented friend, Dustin Gee, who suffered a sudden fatal heart attack at the height of his career.

Christmas was a memorable time too. We discovered the girl living opposite us in the cul-de-sac came from Derry and knew my sister so that produced a good gossip about old times. Then at Mass on Christmas Day, the priest invited all the children to bring their toys up to the altar, and asked them if they knew why we gave presents at Christmas, that it was really Jesus' birthday. It was a scene of great poignancy as they sang "Happy Birthday" to Jesus, and offered the gift of their love to Him.

After an English and then an Irish concert tour during the spring, I was exhausted, and one of my most exciting work opportunities seemed about to be spoilt. I was booked to do some shows on the QE2, but after flying for twenty-four hours to join the ship at Hawaii, I crawled aboard with a perforated eardrum and a chest infection. I felt dreadful. I don't know how, but I managed one show before my voice went completely, and by this time I was not only ill but scared. Scared that some real damage had been done to my vocal chords, scared that the old troubles were returning, for my throat and chest had never felt so bad since that time.

The chaplain on the ship knew how worried I was, and offered the suggestion, rather unhopefully, that a nurse friend of his in Miami where we were heading might know of a throat specialist. For four days we tried to reach her, knowing that no specialist would be able to fit me in at a moment's notice, but we just couldn't get through, so when we actually arrived in Miami, we were running out of hope that anything would come of the chaplain's idea. But when we eventually managed to contact his friend on the phone, we were absolutely amazed, for it turned out that she was working for the top throat specialist in Florida – who actually *specialised* in singers' problems! Not only that, but we discovered that although she had spent the past forty years in America, she had been brought up in the tiny village in Fermanagh where Damien had been born, and had spent most of her childhood in the house where he had grown up, the previous owners before Damien's family having been her foster parents.

It seemed such a staggering set of coincidences that I had an overwhelming sense of God's specific plan working through it all. Unbelievably, this nurse was able to set up an appointment for me at ten o'clock the very next day, and I had a strange feeling that this meeting would be the final piece of jigsaw falling into place.

By midday the picture which had been slowly taking shape since the time of my throat operation was complete. Ever since the problems had started, I had always had a secret fear that my chords were permanently damaged in some subtle way which would reveal itself later, when my voice would just pack up one day and never work again. Somehow I had always felt that if I could possibly *see* my vocal chords in some way, I would be reassured that everything was all right – in the same way, I suppose, as a mother longs for the ultrasound scan which will show her that the unseen baby in her womb is well and growing.

Incredibly, this specialist had a machine which enables you to see your own voice box. By way of tubes with a microscopic camera being passed through my nose I was able to see my vocal chords and actually watch them functioning normally and strongly when I sang. It made all the difference in the world to my confidence as I now know that any throat problems I have are just as mundane as anyone else's, and somehow I feel as if now my voice is a friend instead of an unpredictable stranger. That experience was one of the most beautiful presents from God I could have had and produced a real strengthening in my faith.

After this euphoric experience it was back to England and work. This time a new departure for me – into the world of television advertising – and, in fact, it was a fascinating and really enjoyable experience. Extraordinary how demanding and complicated it can be, spending thirty seconds extolling the virtues of children's toys. I had never realised what a highly pressurised business it is. Precision is the key word. Everything is timed and planned to the minutest detail – not just how you breathe but for how long; how often you blink, and where, exactly, you put your arm or your leg. With about forty-five people examining you as if you were a piece of meat in a butcher's window, it took some getting used to, but I enjoyed the challenge and the opportunity to snatch another small taste of screen acting. Several other commercials followed after that including one for soap! This is an area in which I would like to work further.

Summer 1986 found me back in Torquay with, for the most part, rain-drenched beaches and the ever-resourceful British holidaymakers who squelched doggedly around the Devon beauty spots all day and turned gratefully into the warmth of the theatre each evening, giving the cast an enthusiastic reception which sprang as much as anything from their relief at being able to escape the elements for a while. So, every cloud has a silver lining . . . ! It was, in fact, another very happy season. Jimmy Cricket was there, a great friend, whilst Little and Large were at the other theatre, and they all came to Ruth's birthday party in August.

Through all this, Damien and I had been giving a great deal of thought to my Christian work, as we had a growing feeling that there was a lot more we wanted to do. From Torquay, I flew to Holland to sing at a Catholic Youth Mass, part of an annual retreat attended by several thousand young. The theme was the role of young people in the Church, and after my singing, I was given an interview spot with my good friend Dave Berry (who, from Servant's Art Trust looks after much of my Christian work), in which I was able to talk about the vision and life young people could offer to the Church. It was the first time I had shared my faith with people of another language and the interview was mediated through an interpreter, but I didn't really notice the barrier at all. I wasn't even aware that while the interpreter was relaying my reply to the crowd, I was nodding and murmuring in agreement as if I understood every word. I didn't realise until afterwards that the real reason for the young people's amused response wasn't just the wittiness of what I said!

More Christian work followed, with a very demanding tour of England and Scotland with the John Daniels' band and Nanette Welmans. John is a talented Christian musician and songwriter who also acts as my musical director. In collaboration with him I recorded my first praise and worship album in November on the Kingsway label, a collection of scripture choruses and hymns both old and new. I just loved recording this album as each hymn meant so much to me.

The fact that you can go from something as spiritual as recording a praise album to playing Snow White in a Christmas pantomime, shows that being Christian doesn't mean that you have to shut yourself up in a sterile box and have nothing to do with the "outside" world. My spiritual life is just as important and real to me when I am doing my "secular" work as when I am involved in something directly Christian, in a way *more* so, really, because it provides a perspective and an anchor point in all I do. In fact, the longer I am in showbusiness, the more I realise how much an experience of God's love and direction is desperately needed. There is such pressure and stress in this line of work, so much that can be ugly and sordid in life, that I really wonder now how people do survive without a personal relationship with God.

I think it would be a terrible thing if being a Christian stopped you laughing. I really believe Jesus must have been the most joyful person who ever lived. The "man of sorrows" had also, I'm sure, the richest sense of humour and fun, and I feel that Christians need to shake off the feeling that it's sinful or frivolous to be happy. The run at Oxford was full of laughs. It was a warm and united cast. We all went on a sponsored slim and raised £1,000 towards equipment for a school for the partially hearing in Tonga (those too slim already went on a cigarette diet or a drink fast!). To make it a bit more fun, we got hold of a huge pair of pink plastic pigs' ears and at the end of the week, the member of the company who had been the biggest piggy, and had actually gained weight, was crowned Pig-of-the-Week and had to wear the ears on the walk-down in the finale. In the middle of all this hilarity, I took an evening off to do a big Christian Concert in the Wembley Conference Centre with Cliff Richard, David Grant and Roy Castle.

Life seemed to be going on in a fairly predictable and pleasant pattern, but, unknown to me, a new era was dawning in my career. The key event was a visit to New Orleans in March 1987 to sing at the Southern Regional Catholic Charismatic Conference. Among the participants were Cardinal Law of Boston and Archbishop Hannon of New Orleans. Now, Boston is well known as a very conservative, traditional city as far as religious things go, so it was a big surprise when Cardinal Law asked me to come and sing at a special Youth Mass in the city on Palm Sunday. He hadn't even heard me sing, yet he wanted to rearrange the whole service to provide a more exciting evangelistic challenge to the youth.

On the last night of the conference, I sang "Totus Tuus",

which has always been a very powerful and moving song for me. Someone else also found in it a strong message, as afterwards Archbishop Hannon asked me to return in September and lead the American young people in singing it for the Pope in the Superdome. It was a great honour, but the thing which thrilled me most was the opportunity both these engagements gave me to share my deepening faith in God within my own denomination. As a Catholic I had been saddened but not surprised by the suspicion with which some Christians from other churches viewed me. If it weren't for God's promise that He will build His Church, and that one day He will present her "perfect and without blemish", I would despair about the divisions among Christians. If only Christians could be the ones to lead the way, to reach out across the barriers of form and culture to love their brothers and sisters who worship God in different ways. But it had been one of my biggest regrets that some of the hierarchy of my own denomination often regarded the idea of renewal or "life in the Spirit" with much reservation, even suspicion.

Palm Sunday was only four weeks away, and after the initial flush of enthusiasm at the idea of going to Boston, I lay awake that night wondering what on earth I would sing. Again, God seemed to have that in hand. A friend of ours, Father Harold Cohen, a Jesuit priest in New Orleans, had a sense that this was too, all part of God's plan, and the next day he prayed over Damien and me that we would be given a special song for the occasion. On the plane home, a song seemed to write itself.

As soon as I could, I sat down at the piano, made a tape of the song, and sent it to John Daniels with an urgent request for an arrangement. Under normal circumstances, I would never expect him to arrange and record a song by this instant-soup method – open the packet and pour on boiling water. It usually takes weeks of collaboration to produce a properly arranged song. But time was something we just didn't have, and we prayed that God would inspire John to come up with a perfect arrangement.

I've said before that when some important spiritual event is on the horizon, things have an uncanny knack of going wrong. So often the children seem to get ill when I am planning to go away and once more the old pattern repeated itself. In the four weeks before our return to Boston, I did a whirlwind tour of Liverpool, Birmingham and the Royal Albert Hall with the RTE Orchestra, then crossed the sea to tour Ireland. In the middle of all this, John-James developed severe headaches and stomach cramps. After three courses of antibiotics, he was taken into Newry Hospital for tests. Fortunately I was nearby, only away for the day in Derry recording for television and when I arrived at the hospital in the evening, I found John-James about to be rushed off to the Belfast Children's Hospital as some peculiarity in his blood count had been discovered. The poor wee boy was absolutely terrified, in a lot of pain, and in the confusion all I picked up was that there was an imbalance in his white blood cells. You only have to mention those words and most people's minds immediately turn to one thing: leukaemia. Full of dread, I sat by John-James' side as the ambulance sped through the darkness. On into the night John-James was struggling through barium meals and other tests while I battled with the fear and panic, and tried to trust in God. By morning, the worst worries had been put aside. John-James was suffering from a blockage of the bowel and a perforated eardrum, conditions which didn't require surgery. Three days later he was recovering at home, the scare about his blood count being my own misunderstanding about the body's healthy reaction to infection. Thank God he was fine, and that very day my Irish tour opened.

Without being able to grab one day's rest, the time came to fly back to Boston, and it was only the very morning of our departure that the tape of the song arrived from John Daniels. So I travelled to the Youth Mass without any idea of what the song was going to sound like and with no time to alter or even rehearse it. The whole event seemed to be based on faith. It was to be a large gathering of young people from different areas of the city, and the agenda for a fairly traditional service had been set months before. But after everything had been carefully planned and all the order-of-service sheets printed, Cardinal Law had thrown it all overboard at the New Orleans conference just a month beforehand because he didn't feel it was what God wanted. A very godly man, he sensed the Holy Spirit filling him with deep concern and urgency about the millions of young people who needed to know the reality of God's love. So strong did this feeling become that he was prepared to disrupt the careful planning of hundreds of people and risk criticism and anger to follow God's leading. (In fact, after the Mass, a woman told me privately that she and all her prayer group had felt just the same prompting from the Holy Spirit and had been praying hard that by some miracle Cardinal Law would change his mind about the service.)

The Cardinal had managed to draw together some of the country's biggest names in the religious scene, like John Michael Talbot, a Franciscan brother, who is one of the best-selling Christian singer-songwriters in America, and Cheri O'Neill (daughter of Pat Boone) and her husband Dan who head a big charity for the third world. Apart from a brief telephone link-up when we had volunteered what we wanted to talk about, there was no set theme or message, and I had the dubious privilege of being first on the bill. The song God had given me on the plane had a very strong message in the chorus which was "say 'yes'; say 'yes' to God's call, say 'yes' to His request for your love, your service, your gifts, your time, your money, your life". As I gave my testimony and introduced the song, I found the words just flowing out of me, challenging the young people to commit themselves totally to God, and I felt I should ask them to say "yes" physically by putting up their hand. The response was overwhelming. The cathedral was a forest of raised arms. And remarkably, as the event went on, each participant independently based their contribution on the same theme of saying "yes" to God. We all had the exciting feeling that we were being caught up in a much bigger move of God than we had ever realised, and soon His plan became clearer.

An interesting appendix to this story is that a day or two later my sister Susan spotted a newspaper photograph and exclaimed, "I didn't know the press was at the Boston service". But when we read the caption under the picture of hundreds of young people raising their hands, we discovered it was taken at the youth rally in South America where the Pope had spoken on just the same theme on exactly the same day.

That night we all gathered together for a meal, and the spontaneous question on everyone's lips was how to bring the young people of Boston and of America into a real commitment to God. As Cardinal Law spoke, it was obvious that he had a real love for the youth of his country, and he had the idea to organise a meeting of all the people he felt could provide the answers to how to reach young people with the gospel. The plan was that we should all meet back in Boston for a big meeting ten weeks' later.

This Palm Sunday visit seemed to open up all sorts of doors I had never even imagined. I happened to meet a group of nuns from the Daughters of St Paul, an order started in the 1940s with a particular ministry in the media. They are quite large publishers of religious books, for example. Out of the blue, they asked me to come and see their convent, but I was meant to be flying home that day and I was just about to refuse politely when I had a strong feeling that I should go. Besides, they were so lovely, so earnest, that I didn't really have the heart to say no.

What a surprise was waiting. We discovered they had an incredible twenty-four-track computerised recording and video studio as well as a huge publishing house. Their ministry is to spread the gospel through the media and they had sensed a growing urgency to reach young people through music which was good but Christ-centered too. So they had asked a contractor to build a first-class studio, but, amusingly, being new to the recording world they had no idea of the quality of equipment they possessed or how to use it to its full capacity!

I had never seen such a wonderful set-up, and I was delighted when they asked me if I would consider recording with them. I flew back to England with Damien, wondering if it was all a wild pipe-dream I should just forget about, but the idea wouldn't leave me. My brother John, who has a lot of experience in the technical side of music-making, was asked to fly over to America to look at the studio. He must have thought we were all mad, so ridiculous did the idea seem of these dear sweet sisters sitting on a mega-complex of recording potential. But he went, and was bowled over by what he saw. Success in this business doesn't come simply by having the best equipment, and he carefully explained to the nuns just what commercial recording would involve – all the hassle, the expense, the heartache, the pressure. Did they really want to go ahead? There were wills of steel behind those demure wimples, and without flinching they replied they wanted to do it because they felt it was God's will. So within a few weeks, Krystal Records was formed and an album produced, a compilation of the best tracks from my first Christian albums. The sleeve note was written by Cardinal Law and the album was released in the States to coincide with the Holy Father's visit to New Orleans.

A few weeks later, fifty people assembled for Cardinal Law's "outreach" meeting in Boston, all American except for Damien, my brother John, Susan and me. We were from every background and persuasion, black leaders, white leaders, Hispanic leaders, Catholics, Protestants . . . In fact, we seemed to represent so many different experiences and ideas that initially our hearts sank as we couldn't imagine getting anything agreed, let alone done. Cardinal Law explained that his vision was to produce a blueprint of evangelism in Boston which might be used for other major cities in America, so he asked us to go away that night and think of a plan for reaching the young people of his city with the message of Christ.

We gulped. We secretly shook our heads. But we all did our best. Damien and I sat up far into the night praying and talking, and the next morning the bleary faces showed others had done the same. We were asked to split up into six tables to discuss our plans and then report to the rest of the group. It was then that the miracle started to unfold. Table by table, we all came up with the same thing, point by point. The plan revealed itself in three stages.

1. Bring to Boston people skilled in evangelistic work who would link up with the already existing outreach teams in the city, and concentrate on six months' evangelistic training.
2. Present an event in music, word and testimony which would provide a focal point for commitment.
3. Provide local trained teams who after the event would take over the work of counselling, teaching and supporting the people who had responded to the message.

That morning was one of the most exciting of my life, more so than all the moments of success and achievement in my career. I have never been involved in something I felt so momentous and significant, and I felt as if God had reached down and scooped me up in His arms. I had always wanted to be able to share my faith more deeply within my own Church, and now Cardinal Law was providing the springboard for a powerful outreach to the people who have always been most in my heart – the young. While the evangelistic training gets under way in Boston, I await with anticipation the event which will light the touch paper of the Holy Spirit's revival in Boston's youth.

Since March 1987, the United States has opened up to me. Sometime before, Word had been taken over, and I had ceased recording on that label, so I had thought that my engagements in America would decrease. But now, avenues have presented themselves everywhere. I have appeared on many network TV shows including a national series with my dear friend Father Harold Cohen, not to mention dozens of radio and press interviews both Christian and secular. The Daughters of St Paul are just releasing my album "In the Palm of His Hands" in America, and in the spring of 1988 I am recording a new album with them, and some commercial tracks in Los Angeles.

I had to take a fortnight off my summer season in Blackpool

to attend the September Youth Rally for the Pope in the New Orleans Superdome. About 80,000 young people gathered to meet him, and I had been allocated a whole half hour with them before his arrival to teach them my song, "Totus Tuus", and share a bit about my faith. I went on to sing "Say Yes", and also "Mary's Song" for it seems to me that Jesus' mother is our role model for saying yes to the will of God: "Be it done unto me according to Thy word." My heart was thumping and my hands trembling as I waited to go on, not so much because I was overawed by the occasion but because I knew that what I said in that half hour was so precious, so important. In the weeks beforehand I had found it almost impossible to concentrate my mind on what I would say. I felt I just couldn't trust my own wisdom. The morning of the rally we had to be at the stadium at 7 o'clock, so at 6 o'clock we had a family Mass in the hotel – my mother, grandmother, sister and a few old friends – prayed that the Holy Spirit would speak through me. Minutes before, I still had only the vaguest idea of what I would talk about, and I had to keep on trusting in God that it was all in His hands and He would give me the words. Then, the moment I stood up to sing and speak a tremendous feeling of peace filled me, taking away all my nerves. I spoke about the challenge and cost of commitment to God in my own life, and as we sang "Totus Tuus" all together it became both a prayer and a statement of our devotion to the Lord. It was soon after this that the Pope entered the stadium. He received an incredible welcome from the young people, who stood laughing, singing and cheering as he circled the stadium in his Pope-mobile and waved to the sea of happy faces.

The youth rally was a very moving and magnificent event. Three stages had been erected: a Spanish choir was assembled on one, I on another and the Pope in the centre. First a young girl addressed the Pope on behalf of the youth of America and then he spoke for twenty minutes about the bond between the youth throughout the nations, their common mission to bring the hope of Christ to a lost world. It was a sensitive, impassioned speech. When he finished, I led the young people in singing "Totus Tuus". They stood to sing with me and it is a moment that I shall never forget.

Then the mood changed as a mini mardi gras (for which New Orleans is so famous) filled the stadium with colour, music and dancing. Three floats expressed the young people's sense of their mission to bring light, hope and joy in the darkness, whilst bands in traditional and local costumes brought a sense of celebration to the scene. All round the stadium, the young people were on their feet, cheering and singing, and there was a tremendous sense of unity and love. At last the Pope rose to give the final blessing and his closing words repeated the challenge to say yes to God, for only in laying down our lives for Him, promised the Pope, would we find real freedom. Then suddenly I realised he was stepping down from his stage and coming to take my hand. It was a gesture of much grace and humility, and I was deeply moved.

I joined my family amid a universal air of carnival. I was particularly thrilled to be with them because the presence of my mother and grandmother reflected quite a miracle in itself. Months back in Ireland when I had received the written invitation to sing at the Youth Rally, my mother had been with me, and my immediate response had been to ask her to come with us. Now, my mother is terrified of flying but she swallowed her feelings and bravely said she would come, "only I must ask your granny too!" Granny is ninety-two! But this extraordinary lady's lifelong ambition had been to go to America, and she leapt at the offer without a moment's hesitation. In fact, she proved to be the life and soul of the expedition. She never tired, and her enthusiasm and humour inspired us all. Because of the heat and the distances, we insisted on hiring a wheelchair for her (an indignity she accepted with gracious good spirit considering wild horses wouldn't have got her into one at home) and I shall never forget about a dozen of us, family and friends, crossing one of the main streets of New Orleans with my nephew Phillip, Susan's son, bumping granny over the tramlines at breakneck speed with her hooting with delight like a little girl. Weak with laughter, we arrived at a restaurant for lunch and for hours sat at the table singing all the Irish songs we could think of, while outside wave upon wave of young people flowed through the streets, arms linked, full of joy and life as they sang choruses and hymns. This nostalgic mood continued throughout the next day which was Sunday, and after Mass for twenty-five of us in the home of some friends of ours, we sang round the piano until midnight, finishing with all the old duets Susan and I used to sing when we were young.

When we were young . . . it's not that I feel so very ancient now, not old enough to say "that's my life and now I have only memories to look back on." In a way, I feel this is just the beginning because my vision of what God can do in and through my life is growing every day. And I don't mean success and fame, though obviously confidence, achievement and pleasure in your work are goals everyone seeks. But my real excitement comes from knowing that God has a plan for my life, just as He has for all who want to love and serve Him. This plan certainly isn't my plan and at times I haven't wanted to go that way. There have been moments when I've rebelled, when I have questioned God's wisdom, even wondered if He really cares or knows what He's doing; times of confusion, anxiety and hurt when I've questioned the path down which He seems to be leading me. It seems that the longer we know Him, the more He expects of us, and asks us to walk by faith and not by what we can understand and see. But again and again, I have discovered His way is always best, that what I find at the end of the line is peace and happiness – which, as most people will admit, is what it's really all about.

Knowing God's will means keeping in touch with Him, building a relationship with Him which, just like any other, comes from spending time together. And that's not easy when your life has little structure or routine. As a family, as individuals, prayer is our lifeline. We know that to survive the ups and downs of life, we need to pray and read the Bible together every day, each morning with the children, if possible. When we make ourselves so busy that God gets pushed out of our lives even for a day or two, we notice how easy it is to slip into a human and material way of looking at things so that we forget that divine plan God has for us. Someone once said to me that if you expect life as a Christian to be a bed of roses, then don't forget even roses have thorns, and certainly I've found that my life hasn't been a trouble-free ride. But looking back, I'm able to see that the things which sometimes seemed hardest to bear were, in fact, the greatest blessings because they made me rely on God instead of my own abilities, and through them, perhaps, I've grown as a person both emotionally and spiritually.

New opportunities seem to open themselves up all the time, like the work in America, and the scope for sharing my faith through the structures of my church, but we are learning to live a day at a time. One very important area of involvement for Damien and me is with the Society for the Protection of the Unborn Child (SPUC). It's a cause close to our hearts, feeling as we do that children are a gift from God as is life itself. We feel that society has a duty to defend its most defenceless member, the unborn baby, remembering always that there are two victims of abortion. Medical science is only just beginning to realise the terrible psychological, and often physical damage caused to the mother. As one mother told me, every time she saw a children's birthday party she thought of how old her child would be, and I myself could cry at the thought of all the millions of wasted lives. My work gives me a platform from which I can voice the protest against this inhumanity to man, and although I'm not a political person, I'm not afraid to use my position to oppose moral and spiritual violations of God's laws.

At the same time, we feel happy for me to continue my professional career. There have been so many elements in my career which could have spelt disaster – like the long lay-off with illness; marriage; children; my Christian involvement – yet it has always picked up and even flourished. But I wouldn't sacrifice my family life or my faith in God for success or money. There's no attraction to me in recording all the time, jetting all over the world to do promotion and working fifty-two weeks a year for fame and fortune. But I do love my work, and when I find it's keeping me away from the children, I try to see it as an investment for time with them in the future.

People do ask me if I feel any conflict between my career and my family. Well, I often wish I could spend more time with them, and obviously everyone would like to be in the ideal position of being able to do the work they enjoy just when it suits. As much as possible we take the children with us if we are going to be away for more than just a day or two, but whenever we are separated we try and phone them every day. But the Lord knows how I feel and I try to be open to God if He wants me to spend less time working. In the meantime, we trust Him, for we are trying to do what we feel He wants us to and we believe that He will protect the children from any harm and insecurity. More than anything else I want them to have a personal knowledge of His love for them. If they wanted to go into show business I wouldn't stop them, but I certainly wouldn't push them, and I would like to make sure that they had a good education so that they wouldn't have to be tied to it if things didn't work out. Grace, Ruth and John-James have beautiful little voices (although I don't always think so when they are arguing) and we just pray that God will use that gift for His glory and for their happiness. And it *is* a great gift and privilege to make music and entertain people, but it is honestly a far greater one for me to have the peace and love of God in my heart.

As for my own personal ambitions, being a Christian doesn't mean having no aims or goals. It's just that our motivation hopefully becomes less selfish. I would love to make an album of Christian songs for children. Children love to sing, therefore music is a wonderful vehicle for conveying to children that faith in God is something that is creative and fun. Music draws them into an experience of the joy and excitement which is, I think, the heart of the Gospel.

One day I hope I will get to Australia. That's not a very spiritual ambition, is it?! Damien's last surviving aunt lives out there, and she has never seen our children. Against all hope and expectation, she managed to get to our wedding, and it would mean so much to us all to be able to make the same journey for her. This strong sense of family is very important to us, as indeed I feel it is with all Irish people: I feel the disintegration of the extended family unit (which includes grandparents and cousins, aunts and uncles) is, in part, responsible for many of the social ills we see today. So whatever we do, whether in my secular or Christian work, Damien and I feel it is a basic principle that the family should come first.

To talk openly about my faith and thoughts is something I still don't find easy. I suppose basically I'm quite a private person and the last thing I want is to appear arrogant and dogmatic. I wouldn't want to abuse the privilege of having an audience by forcing my beliefs on them. There are many things I don't understand about the way God works, and in the realms of theology I'm out of my depth, but I do know His love and power are very real and I would like to share that through my music and in this book without people feeling threatened or preached at. I probably won't succeed all the time. Even Christians can feel threatened by the way others express their faith, but if I can just be a channel of the love God has shown me, if I could just fulfil something of what He put me on this earth to do, then it would mean far more to me than any worldly success.

Cliff Richard

You, Me and Jesus

Cliff Richard's personal introduction to the Bible. For all those who are intrigued by his faith and for anyone who really wants to understand him, here is the essential Cliff Richard.

Speaking from his heart and out of his own experience, Cliff comments on over 100 passages from the Bible. In his own honest, informal, down-to-earth way he explains their relevance to all of us in today's world.

'What I've written is what I've learned and, I promise you, that's only a scratch on the surface. There's so much more, and what I'd love this book to be is a kind of appetite-whetter, that will cause you to study the Bible for yourself and delve far deeper.'

(Cliff Richard in his Introduction)

You, Me and Jesus is illustrated throughout with witty line drawings by John Farman and contains eight pages of black and white photographs.

Cliff Richard

Jesus, Me and You

What does the Bible say about how we should live as Christians in today's world? In *Jesus, Me and You* Cliff draws on eighty passages from both Old and New Testaments, and in his own witty and thought-provoking style unearths some sound advice and good sense concerning modern living. Ideal for use as a springboard to daily Bible study, or for simply dipping into, *Jesus, Me and You* is illustrated throughout with lively cartoons plus a sixteen-page section of colour photographs.

'It's refreshing, exciting, funny, stimulating.' *The Officer*

'Fans of all ages will enjoy *Jesus, Me and You*.' *Christian Family*

Sheila Walsh

God Put a Fighter in Me

A new edition, bringing Sheila's story right up to date

Battalions of darkness rise above me,
But God put a fighter in me, a fighter in me.
So we will sing songs of victory,
We will rise and set men free . . .

These lines, from a song composed for Sheila by Graham Kendrick, set the tone for this autobiography now published as a Hodder Christian Paperback with an additional chapter and new photographs.

Sheila takes a wry look at herself, her hopes, expectations and fears as she steps out into the limelight and explains how a shy, young Scottish girl, afraid of personal relationships, became an outgoing, popular Gospel singer, rock star and TV presenter. Her warmth, vivacity, deep faith and genuine concern for others all shine through.

Sheila Walsh, with six major albums to her name, now spends most of her time touring internationally.

Recordings By Dana

IN THE PALM OF HIS HAND
Record & Cassette SFR/SFC156

Dana's beautiful renditions of some of today's most popular worship songs, including 'Make me a channel of Your peace', 'Freely, freely', and 'Living under the shadow of His wing', together with some that are less well known including Dana's own 'Richer than gold'.

Produced and arranged by John Daniels.

NO GREATER LOVE
Cassette only KMC482

Songs include 'Totus Tuus (Totally Yours)', 'Mary's song (I rocked Him as a baby)', and 'Let there be love'. Recorded in the United States, this album brings together the best from her first two gospel albums.

'A selection of songs that reveal her depth as a woman of faith' –

Bernard Law
Archbishop of Boston

Both these recordings are published by Kingsway and are available from your local Christian Bookshop, or in case of difficulty direct from: The Rainbow Company, PO Box 77, Hailsham, E. Sussex BN27 3EF.